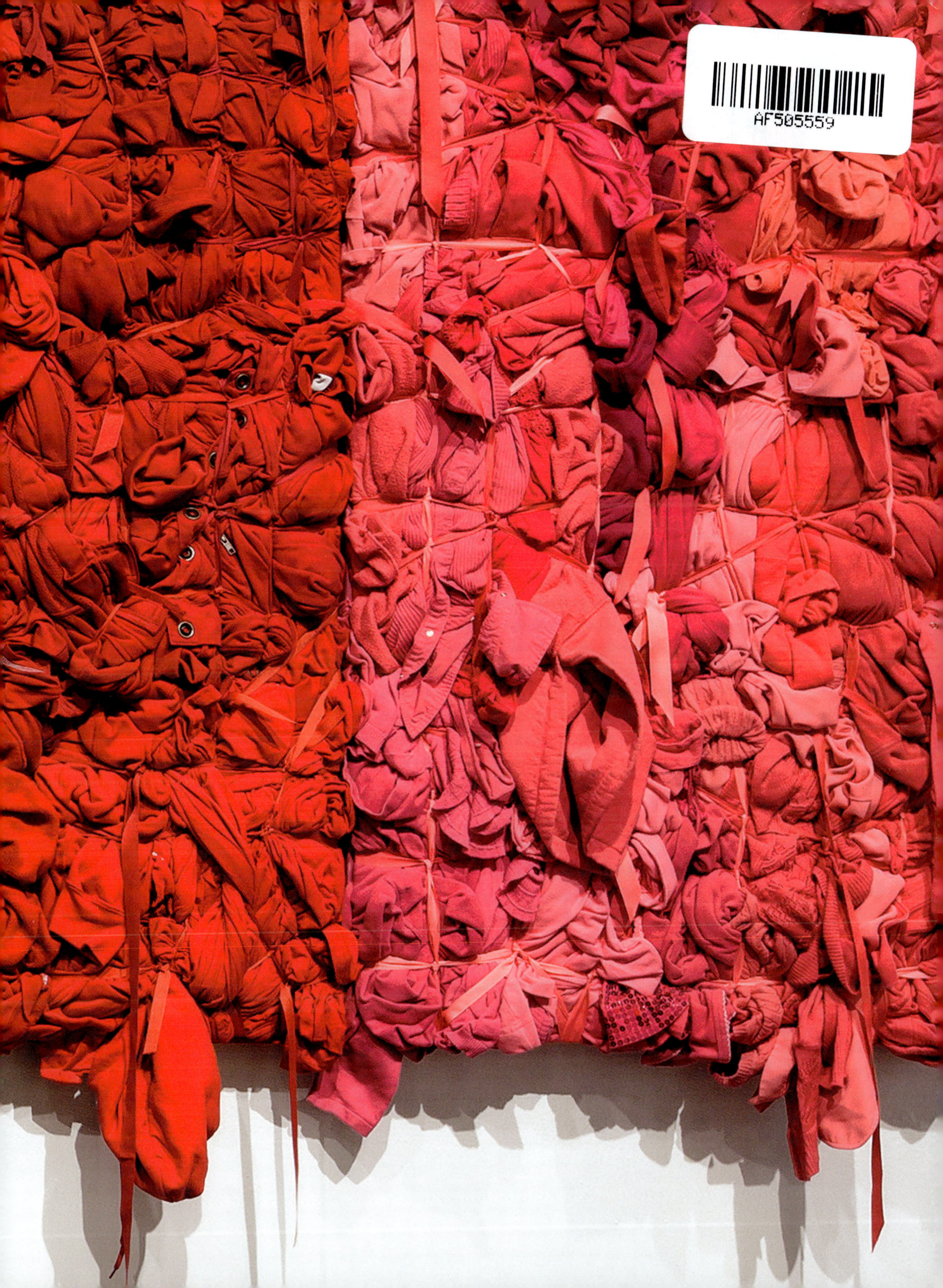
AF505559

SHINIQUE SMITH
Wonder and Rainbows

First printing 2016

Library of Congress Cataloging-in-Publication Data

Names: Delmez, Kathryn E. | Mergel, Jen. | Smith, Shinique, 1971– | Frist Center for the Visual Arts (Nashville, Tenn.), organizer.
Title: Shinique Smith : wonder and rainbows / editor, Kathryn E. Delmez ; contributors, Kathryn E. Delmez, Jen Mergel, Shinique Smith.
Description: Nashville, Tennessee : Frist Center for the Visual Arts, 2016. | "Published in association with two exhibitions organized by the Frist Center for the Visual Arts: Shinique Smith: Wonder and Rainbows, October 9, 2015–January 10, 2016, Gordon Contemporary Artists Project Gallery; Found Narratives, June 10–September 18, 2016, Conte Community Arts Gallery." | Includes bibliographical references.
Identifiers: LCCN 2016030291 | ISBN 9780826521583 (pbk. : alk. paper)
Subjects: LCSH: Smith, Shinique, 1971– Exhibitions. | Smith, Shinique, 1971– Interviews.
Classification: LCC N6537.S6178 A4 2016 | DDC 709.2–dc23
LC record available at https://lccn.loc.gov/2016030291

ISBN-13: 978-0-826-52158-3 (paper)

Book Designer: Kristina Colucci
Copy Editor: Peg Duthie
Managing Editor: Wallace Joiner
Typeset in Bickham Script and Univers
Printed on Athens Silk
Printed by Lithographics, Inc., Nashville

Book sponsored in part by the Friends of Contemporary Art:

Anonymous
Claiborne Blevins
Susan H. Edwards
Jennifer and Billy Frist
Bob and Julie Gordon
Frank and Gwen Gordon
Jeff and Gail Jacobs
Neil Krugman and Lee Pratt
Luke and Susan Simons
Hope and Howard Stringer

Published in association with two exhibitions organized by the Frist Center for the Visual Arts:

Shinique Smith: Wonder and Rainbows
October 9, 2015–January 10, 2016
Gordon Contemporary Artists Project Gallery

Found Narratives
June 10–September 18, 2016
Conte Community Arts Gallery
Presenting Sponsor

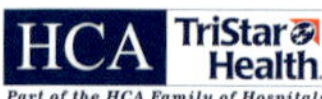

Supporting Sponsors

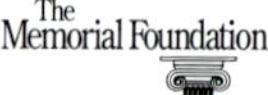 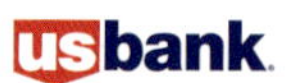

The Frist Center for the Visual Arts is supported in part by

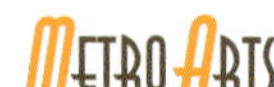 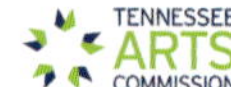 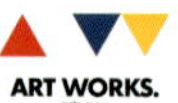

Cover: detail, *Inner Clock*, plate 1. Inside front cover: detail, *Black/Blue/Green/Yellow/Orange/Red/Pink*, plate 15. i: detail, *Somewhere out there (in here)*, plate 2. iii: *Open Word Lattice (Black & Rainbow)* (installation view, Frist Center), plate 8. Photo: John Schweikert. 14: detail, *Tiny Dancer*, plate 3. 50: detail, *Splendid*, plate 20. 88: detail, *The Oldest Love*, plate 34. Inside back cover: *Arcadian Clusters* (installation view, Eli and Edythe Broad Art Museum at Michigan State University), 2014. Site-specific mixed-media installation. Photo: Charlie Edwards

EDITOR

Kathryn E. Delmez

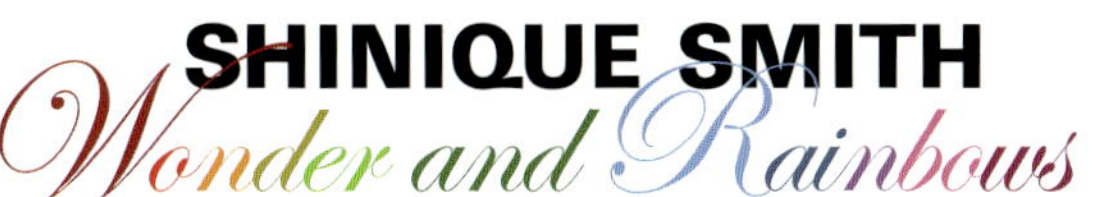

SHINIQUE SMITH
Wonder and Rainbows

CONTRIBUTORS

Kathryn E. Delmez

Jen Mergel

Shinique Smith

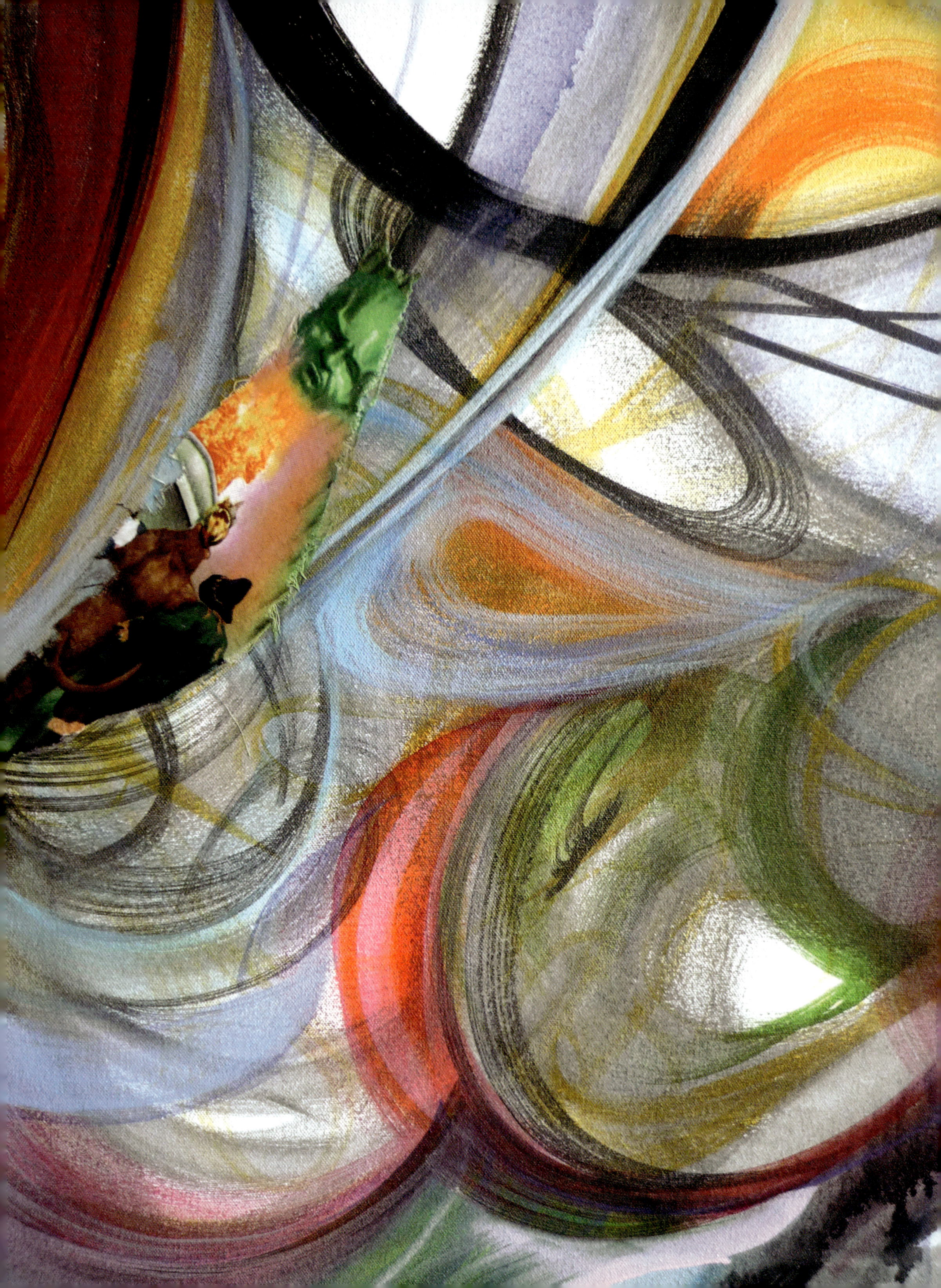

Contents

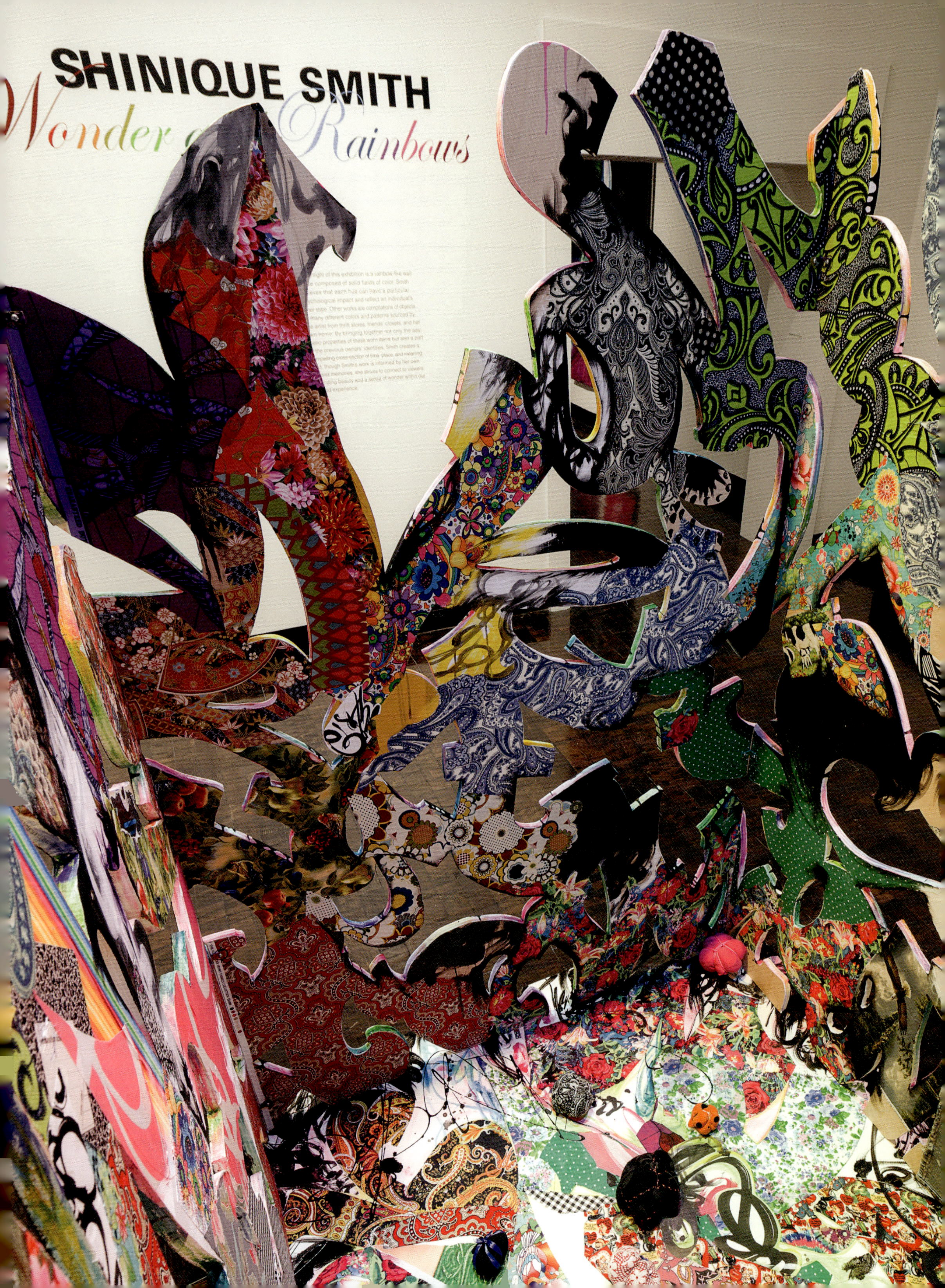

SHINIQUE SMITH
Wonder and Rainbows

Foreword

$\mathscr{B}$eginning in the fall of 2013, the Frist Center began a relationship with Shinique Smith that has deepened over the years to inspire the publication of this book, a lasting document of our esteem. Her work has been presented at the Frist Center almost continuously over the past three years. Smith was one of the artists in *30 Americans*, a touring exhibition drawn from the Rubell Family Collection in Miami. Intrigued by Smith's two sculptures in that exhibition, the Frist Center curator in charge of *30 Americans*, Kathryn Delmez, subsequently organized *Shinique Smith: Wonder and Rainbows*, a 2015 solo show in the Gordon Contemporary Artists Project Gallery.

During the preparation of *Wonder and Rainbows*, Frist Center educators Shaun Giles and Rosemary Brunton initiated a collaborative project with local teaching artists that would result in *Found Narratives*, a 2016 exhibition inspired by Smith's work. In October 2015, members of Frist Center community partner organizations met with Smith to learn more about her practice and share personal experiences with one another; then, guided by the teaching artists, they incorporated discarded items as well as conventional craft materials into the new and different histories they fashioned during the collaboration. The works showcased in the Conte Community Arts Gallery were created by artists from Maplewood High School, led by Stephanie Pruitt; Poverty & the Arts, led by Courtney Adair Johnson; Thistle Farms, led by Gail Looper; and YMCA Latino Achievers, led by Amber Lelli. Johnson, Looper, and Pruitt were assisted by former Frist Center intern Eva Young.

Smith has been widely acclaimed as one of the leading artists of her generation. Her success has been sufficiently gradual to nurture personal and professional gravitas. She is innately visual and talented, seeing the world around her as raw material and meaningful inspiration. Smith is curious and intrepid. Since childhood, she has defined and orchestrated the wonder of a rich visual imagination. Her mind's eye sees possibilities in a wide range of influences, from fashion to philosophy, poetry to rainbows. Smith finds voice as a painter, sculptor, and installation artist. By exceeding the limits, breaking the barriers, and embracing wonder, Smith inspires us to look at our world in new ways.

Susan H. Edwards, PhD
Executive Director and CEO

Acknowledgments

This book provides background on Shinique Smith's training and career as well as insight into her philosophical, spiritual, and theoretical interests. We thank Kathryn Delmez for her introduction. She has been a steadfast champion of Smith's work and a relentless advocate for the publication of this book. Jen Mergel, the Robert L. Beal, Enid L. Beal and Bruce A. Beal Senior Curator of Contemporary Art at the Museum of Fine Arts, Boston, curated *Shinique Smith: Bright Matter* at her institution in 2014; we thank her for her insightful conversation with the artist. Smith has been a generous colleague throughout our association. We thank her for her cooperation at every turn. Her words are as revelatory as her art. We appreciate her responses to Jen Mergel as well as her own written contribution to this book. The artist would further like to acknowledge Pamela Joyner for her continuous support, and Gary Pennock, Vkara Phifer-Smith, and the Smith family for their ceaseless contributions to her life and work.

We are indebted to individuals and organizations who have been dedicated supporters of Smith and of the Frist Center's role in bringing greater visibility to her work in the Mid-South, including the Frist Center's Friends of Contemporary Art; its board of trustees, especially Billy Frist, president and chair; the Metro Nashville Arts Commission; the Tennessee Arts Commission; and the National Endowment for the Arts. The arrangements for *Wonder and Rainbows* would not have been possible without David Castillo, Smith's representative at David Castillo Gallery. For lending art to the Frist Center, we thank Christopher Dlutowski and Peter Occolowitz, and Francie Bishop Good and David Horvitz. Our entire staff contributed in myriad ways to the success of the exhibition, and we extend particular thanks to the late Michael Brechner, exhibition designer; Kristina Colucci, senior graphic designer; and Richard Feaster, registrar.

Found Narratives likewise would not have been possible without our sponsors, partners, and staff. We are extremely grateful to presenting sponsor HCA and TriStar Health and supporting sponsors The Memorial Foundation and U.S. Bank Foundation. For their participation in *Found Narratives*, we acknowledge Maplewood High School, Poverty & the Arts, Thistle Farms, and YMCA Latino Achievers. For their leadership and artistic direction, we thank Courtney Adair Johnson, Amber Lelli, Gail Looper, and Stephanie Pruitt. Additional thanks go to Rosemary Brunton, Shaun Giles, Hans Schmitt-Matzen, and Eva Young.

For the production of this book, we again acknowledge Kathryn Delmez, who served as editor as well as contributor. Michael Ames, the director of Vanderbilt University Press, is a loyal friend of the Frist Center who responds with enthusiasm to our publishing requests. We thank him for ensuring the distribution of this book. At the Frist Center, we thank Kristina Colucci for her thoughtful and sensitive design, managing editor Wallace Joiner for shepherding this book through fits and starts to reach a successful result, and copy editor Peg Duthie for her expertise and unflappable patience. We also gratefully acknowledge the assistance of project coordinator Kim Boyer and curatorial intern Lucy Kwabah Mensah.

Our greatest debt is, of course, to Shinique Smith.

—*S. H. E.*

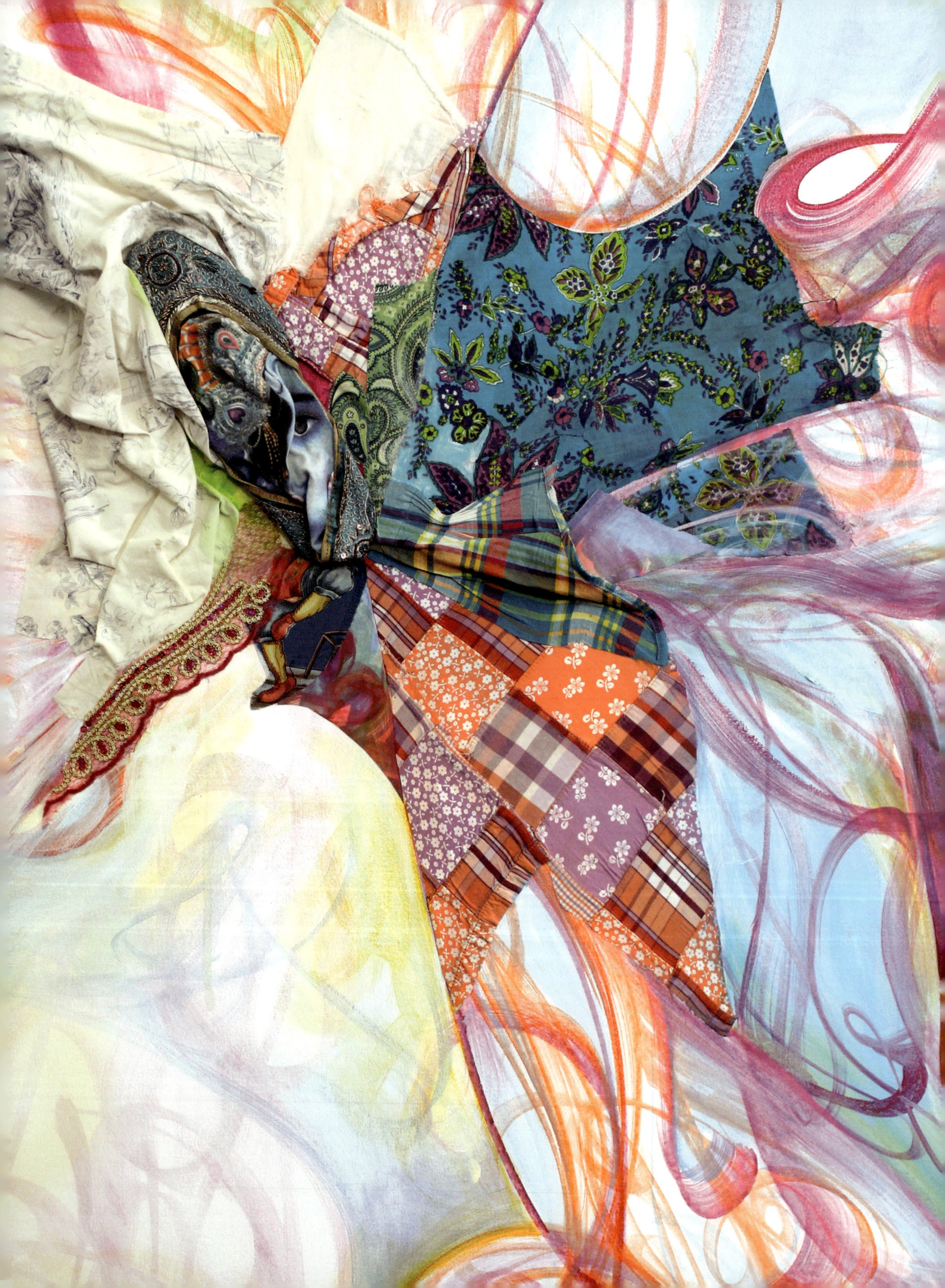

Introduction

Kathryn E. Delmez
Curator
Frist Center for the Visual Arts

Like spiral galaxies composed of millions of orbiting stars, the works of New York–based artist Shinique Smith are graceful yet forceful combinations of many different materials and ideas. The wide range of inspirations that inform her practice includes dance, Eastern spiritual philosophies, fashion, music, art history, childhood wonder, graffiti, Japanese calligraphy, and poetry. Smith's sculptures, which either hang from the ceiling or sit directly on the floor, are made by binding together with knotted cords and ribbons an array of textiles, typically old clothing, sourced from multiple locations. Tucked within the folds of fabric are seemingly unimportant items from everyday life such as artificial flowers, butterfly decals, or stuffed animals. In Smith's paintings, these elements intermingle with cloth fragments, bold calligraphic brushwork, and vivid waves of color to create energetic expressions of her personal history as well as a greater sense of cultural concern and cosmic connectivity.

Smith attributes many facets of her work to the broad scope of experiences she was exposed to as a child. Her creativity was fostered from a young age and she studied ballet, theater, and drawing throughout her youth in Baltimore. Smith's mother, then a fashion designer and magazine editor, often brought her to fabric stores and fashion shows. Deeply involved in esoteric spiritual groups, Smith's mother also took her to the Tibetan Meditation Center. The artist remembers meeting the Dalai Lama there and falling asleep amid the sounds of people chanting and bells ringing. Smith is an only child and often relied on her own imagination to pass the time. She states, "Drawing, making art, setting up play schools and pretend situations . . . that aspect of play, feeling of discovery, using your imagination with objects, playing by yourself and making up things, still affects my work today."[1] Additionally, Smith notes the influence of the physical environment of her childhood, recalling that her grandmother "would mix brocades and florals with plaids and patterns that didn't seemingly belong together [in her home], but they would harmonize. . . . My surroundings influenced me when I was a child, as they do now. I find magic in the relationships of objects and the people that surround me."[2]

Demonstrating artistic skills, Smith was accepted into the competitive Baltimore School of the Arts at the age of twelve. Like Jean-Michel Basquiat, she wrote graffiti during high school, and suggestions of popular culture and expressive lines remain a fundamental part of Smith's work, although she now regards direct references to tagging as a nostalgic recollection of her youth.[3] In 2001, after spending time on the West Coast as a costume designer for major motion pictures and running an international Black film festival, she returned to Baltimore and the Maryland Institute College of Art, where she had received a BFA in 1992.[4] Her graduate thesis explored writing as a form of meditation and the relationship between graffiti and the more rarified field of Japanese calligraphy, a subject she had studied as an undergraduate. She posits that "in both you can't back up, you must have a confident hand when you put your brush to the surface. There's no erasing."[5] The vigorous handstyle found in her paintings today is a fusion not only of graffiti and calligraphy, but also of the dramatic gestures and delicate drips of Franz Kline, Joan Mitchell, and Jackson Pollock.

Shinique Smith first earned national critical attention through the 2005 exhibition *Frequency*, a survey of emerging African American artists at the Studio Museum in Harlem that also included Nick Cave, Xaviera Simmons, and Hank Willis Thomas. For this show and its 2001 precursor, *Freestyle,* curator Thelma Golden used the term "post-black" to describe a generation of artists who came of age after the civil rights movement and are "both post-Basquiat and post-Biggie."[6] To varying degrees, these artists may refer to issues related to the complexity of "blackness" or black identity in their work, but do so within a wide spectrum of contemporary aesthetic and social concerns.[7] Around this time, Smith began to focus on a body of work in which she binds an assortment of worn clothing and accessories into large rectangular bundles (see plates 21 and 33). The "Bale Variants" extend an art historical lineage of important mileposts, such as Robert Rauschenberg's "Combine" sculptures of found objects and the Minimalist use of the cube and the grid as an underlying structural base (figure 1). Formally, the bales express Smith's life-long attraction to fashion, textiles, and pattern and her aim to create a visually compelling composition in which each component, with its own properties and history, becomes subsumed within the larger whole, like individuals in society. But they also reflect her concern about the culture of excess and waste that permeates wealthy nations. The series was inspired by an article in the *New York Times Magazine* that documented the shipment of massive machine-compressed blocks of unwanted clothing from the United States to impoverished countries.[8] It specifically followed the path of a University of Pennsylvania T-shirt, which had been donated to a secondhand store by a woman living on Manhattan's Upper East Side and eventually reached a man in West Africa who bought it for $1.20. Smith sees the transatlantic commercial exchange of this material object, discarded by one person and valued by another, as an overlooked connection between two people who would otherwise have no point of contact.

Smith also recognizes the significance that apparel holds as a reflection of aspects of the owner's identity and personal life. Clothing is a relatively timeless and universal mode of presenting one's gender, socioeconomic position, age, ethnicity, and even religion or occupation. People often make assumptions about others based on what they wear (consider the bias assigned to someone dressed as a stereotypical businessperson, hippie,

Fig. 1
Robert Rauschenberg (American, 1925–2008). *Bed*, 1955. Oil and pencil on pillow, quilt and sheet on wood supports, 75 1/4 x 31 1/2 x 8 in. The Museum of Modern Art, New York, Gift of Leo Castelli in honor of Alfred H. Barr, Jr. © VAGA, NY. Digital image © The Museum of Modern Art/ Licensed by SCALA /Art Resource, NY

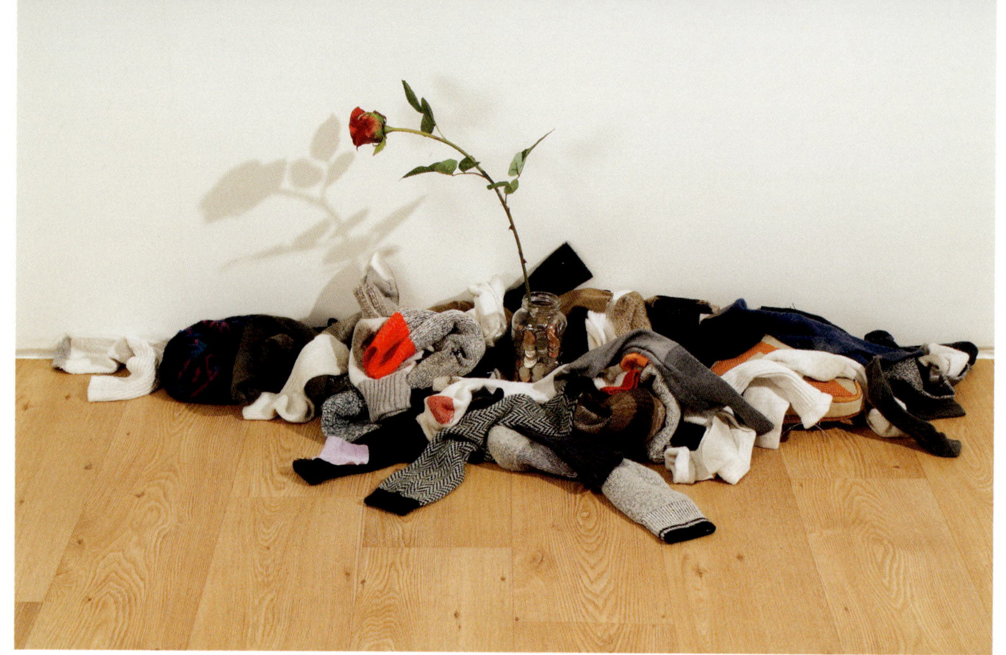

cowboy, or hip-hop star). In addition to apparel's role in constructing an image, Smith
is interested in the memories and histories associated with attire. She sees a cast-off
garment to be like a skin shed by a snake: the imprint of the wearer is still there and a
part of his or her energy remains. By reusing old items in her bales, hanging bundles,
and collaged paintings, Smith gives them new purpose and advances their journey.
Some "donors" of the materials Smith uses are unknown, while others are close
family members and friends. At times, the artist includes textiles that once belonged
to cherished loved ones who have passed away, thereby extending Smith's memory
of them. Clothing can also represent a particular phase in one's life. Smith reuses
meaningful objects from her own past, such as a dress she wore to many art events
and an ex-boyfriend's shirts and socks (figure 2). Evocative of both her life and the
histories of others, each random yet carefully selected assortment of belongings
creates a "cross section of time, place, and meaning."[9]

Making something out of what many would regard as nothing gives Smith a sense
of discovery that harkens back to the creativity of her youth, when she played with
whatever was at hand. Her work often contains objects associated with girlhood:
glittery fairy wings, dollhouses, the tulle of ballet tutus, and toys associated with
the 1970s and '80s—the decades of her youth—such as Care Bears, Cabbage
Patch Kids, Barbie dolls, and My Little Ponies. By unapologetically featuring
these products—kitschy to some, beloved by others—in "high" art shown in major

museums and galleries, Smith elevates and brings visibility to the often trivialized experiences of young girls. In doing so, she also counters a jarring assertion by an acquaintance who had said that "Black girls don't frolic."[10] The transition from little girl to teenager is referenced by such items as ripped jeans, deflated Mylar birthday balloons, composition books, hair accessories, and even a beanbag on which a young girl might lounge while listening to music or hanging out with a friend. These objects represent a range of childhood memories, from the magical moments in which whimsy and fantasy are embraced before the confines of adulthood set in, to the inevitable and at times uncomfortable journey of self-discovery that accompanies growing up.

Giving objects new life and imbuing her work with their essence relate to Smith's spiritual leanings, which, like her art, braid together multiple strands. She is intrigued by the metaphysical realm and the nature of how people, objects, and the universe intersect. She believes that truths may be revealed though the study of astrology, numerology, auras, and cosmic energy. For example, when she had her aura documented through Kirlian photography during a time when she was grieving over the loss of a family member, the photograph was primarily red. During more balanced times, it was a rainbow (see page 81), which has been a source of inspiration and personal curiosity for Smith.[11] Since childhood, Smith has been intrigued by cultural myths and legends—Greek and Roman, Celtic, Native American, and Maori—and maintains that, as expressed in Joseph Campbell's book *The Power of Myth* (1988), a line of truth runs through and connects different times and cultures. Smith was exposed to multiple belief systems as a young girl and vividly recalls in her home a laughing Buddha, a Jewish mezuzah, an illustrated book on Krishna, and a copy of Max Ehrmann's "Desiderata" (1927). Although she does not consider herself a subscriber to a specific religion, she is drawn to many Buddhist and Hindu philosophical concepts, especially those regarding the impermanence and the cyclical nature of the material world. The mandala form, a symbol of the universe in Buddhist and Hindu traditions and a tool in meditation, often appears or is suggested by the strong centrality in her work. From a dense core, an often cacophonous array of elements radiates, reflecting her desire for a balance between order and chaos.

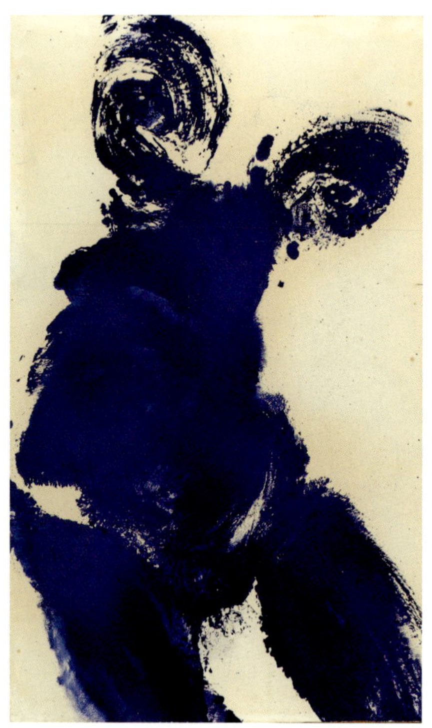 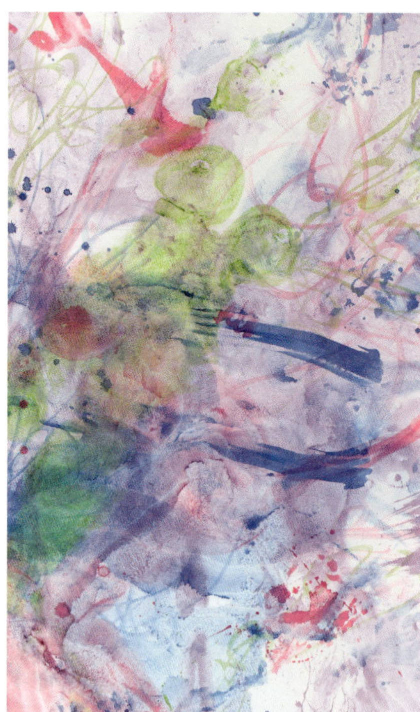

Like the abstract artist Agnes Martin, Smith sees the creative process as a ritualistic journey and the resulting objects as having a spiritual dimension.[12] She is meticulous about what she collects, selecting only objects that have "a particular color or pattern, a relationship to a utopian ideal, something whimsical."[13] Much time is spent sourcing the materials from thrift shops, dollar stores, her own home, and the homes of her family and friends. She then methodically organizes the items in her studio according to color and pattern. Smith speaks of the physical strength and the mantra-like repetition required from her body to tie together—over and over—the many elements in her sculptures, and the broad gestural movement needed to make the large waves and lines of her paintings. The transfer of energy between the artist and the work has a metaphysical dimension: "So much of my work is about my touch. . . . Everything has to emanate from me."[14] Smith believes that the energy she imbues her work with is then channeled to the viewer and "it becomes full from the experience of others looking at it."[15]

Although Smith's paintings and sculptures are generally abstract, the human body is alluded to in various manifestations. On one end of the spectrum, it is sensed as the absence of the bodies of the previous owners of the clothing, including hers. For example, anatomical contours appear in *Soul Elsewhere*, a sculpture made from the artist's work jeans in which the curves of her hips are apparent (plate 29). Smith has also used her body to apply paint to a canvas or wall, leaving a visible imprint in a manner similar to Ana Mendieta, David Hammons, or Yves Klein (figures 3 and 4). Finally, she uses her own body in performance pieces such as *Bundle Me*, in which she explores what it might be like to be inside one of her sculptures.

In recent years, particularly after Smith moved to a pastoral retreat near the Catskill area of the Hudson Valley, nature has played a larger role in her creativity.[16] She has become re-invested in color, which she had consciously stripped from her practice for a period, beginning in 2001. In 2009, she created a multipaneled wall piece composed of found fabrics sorted and arranged into five solid fields of color: blue, green, yellow, orange, and red.[17] Initially inspired by the "spectrum" paintings of Minimalist artist Ellsworth Kelly and the optical experiments of Josef Albers, it is meant to represent a range of both hue and emotion. Like Wassily Kandinsky, who espoused similar theories in his treatise *Concerning the Spiritual in Art* (1912), Smith believes that each color can have a particular psychological impact and can reflect an individual's inner state (figure 5). Since reintroducing color as a primary subject, she has also "embraced rainbows, butterflies and a plethora of symbols that connect to my youth, my femininity and the violent and romantic struggle of life."[18] Smith reframes these often clichéd symbols of girlhood innocence and presents them as signifiers of more serious-minded and universal concepts. For example, rainbows are not merely a pretty decorative motif, but can represent unrestrained dreams, harmony after turbulent times, diversity, and, especially in the wake of the 2015 Supreme Court ruling on gay marriage, political equality. Smith notes that although we learn how and why rainbows form as children, adults often feel a sense of awe when they encounter their beauty, and poets and songwriters have long mused about what is at the end of these still mysterious and fleeting phenomena.[19] Butterflies likewise can symbolize something more philosophical, as they morph into entirely new forms at different stages of life. Fragile and simple as young caterpillars, they build their cocoons and emerge as new creatures with beautiful and colorful wings that allow

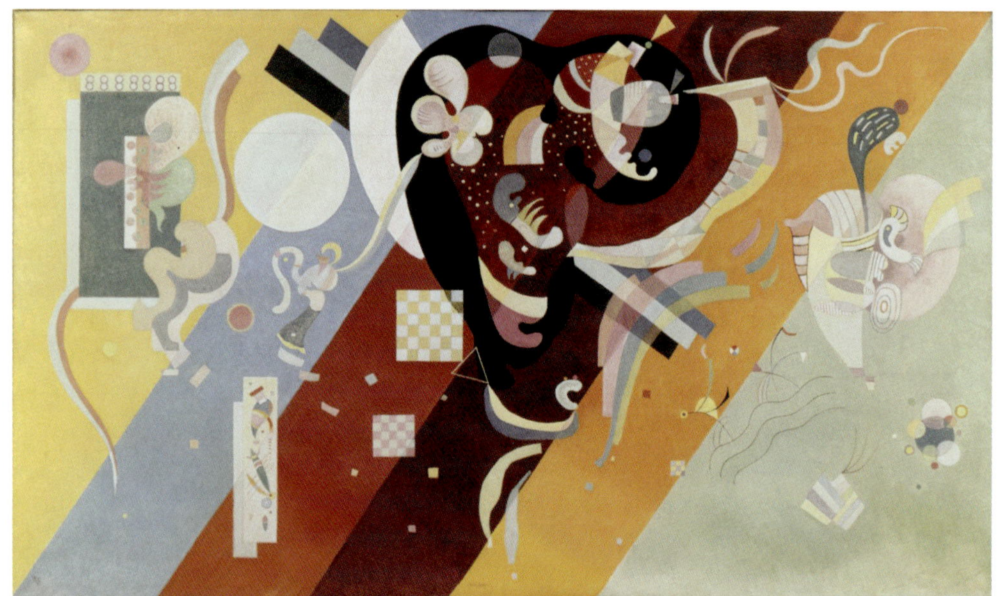

them to fly (a wondrous transformation that many children discover at a very young age through Eric Carle's ubiquitous 1969 book *The Very Hungry Caterpillar*). To Smith, this transformation is "profound to any human being struggling to evolve in this world and in particular to any marginalized person."[20]

Through her emotionally and visually exuberant work, Shinique Smith channels and hopes to transfer to viewers the sense of wonder and discovery she cherishes from her childhood. Her installations often use all six surfaces of an exhibition space (employing the ceiling and floor in addition to the walls), creating an engaging aura of enchantment. Many objects simultaneously seem to represent teeming microcosms and macrocosms: are they telescopic pictures of galaxies or microscopic views of cells? Though Smith's artistic practice is informed by her own identity and memories, she strives to connect to viewers by drawing attention to the beauty within our shared experience. Ultimately, the kaleidoscope-like sculptures and paintings are meant to convey a universal appreciation of life, both in its pain and sweetness.

Notes

1. Michael Huebner, "Shinique Smith Creating Art 'Etched in Collective History' at Birmingham Museum of Art," *AL.com*, August 14, 2013.

2. An earlier version of this quote appeared in "Dynamic Display—*Shinique Smith: Firsthand*," interview by Sarah Jesse, *Unframed*, February 6, 2013, unframed.lacma.org.

3. Barbara Pollack, "Clothes Connections," *ARTnews,* January 2010.

4. Smith now serves as a member of the Maryland Institute College of Art's Board of Trustees.

5. An earlier version of this quote appeared in Hilarie M. Sheets, "Giving Castoffs a Second Life," *New York Times*, March 7, 2013, nytimes.com.

6. Christine Y. Kim and Franklin Sirmans, *Freestyle* (New York: Studio Museum in Harlem, 2001).

7. For a discussion on Thelma Golden's development of the concept of "post-black" art, see Thelma Golden and Christine Y. Kim, *Frequency* (New York: Studio Museum in Harlem, 2005).

8. George Packer, "How Susie Bayer's T-shirt Ended Up on Yusuf Mama's Back," *New York Times Magazine*, March 31, 2002.

9. "Dynamic Display."

10. Shinique Smith, conversation with the author, December 2014.

11. This photograph has been a source of inspiration and personal curiosity for the artist as she reflects on her work and who she is in the world.

12. Ryan McClure, "Shinique Smith: All You Need Is Love," *Whitewall,* March 6, 2013, whitewallmag.com.

13. "Dynamic Display."

14. Marina Cashdan, "Care Bears and My Little Pony: Shinique Smith's Brooklyn Treasure Trove," *Huffington Post*, September 13, 2010, huffingtonpost.com.

15. McClure, "Shinique Smith."

16. Smith notes, "I think the inspiration [of nature] was always there, but moving just allowed me to focus on it. . . . You can't always pause to have a musing thought on the way a flower opens." Nadiah Fellah, "Shinique Smith Discusses Her New Show at James Cohan Gallery," *New American Paintings*, February 27, 2013.

17. Smith created a new version of *Blue/Green/Yellow/Orange/Red* for her 2015 exhibition at the Frist Center, adding a black panel to one end and a hot pink panel to the other (see plate 15)

18. Shinique Smith, e-mail to the author, December 18, 2014.

19. Shinique Smith, e-mail to the author, June 11, 2015.

20. Ibid.

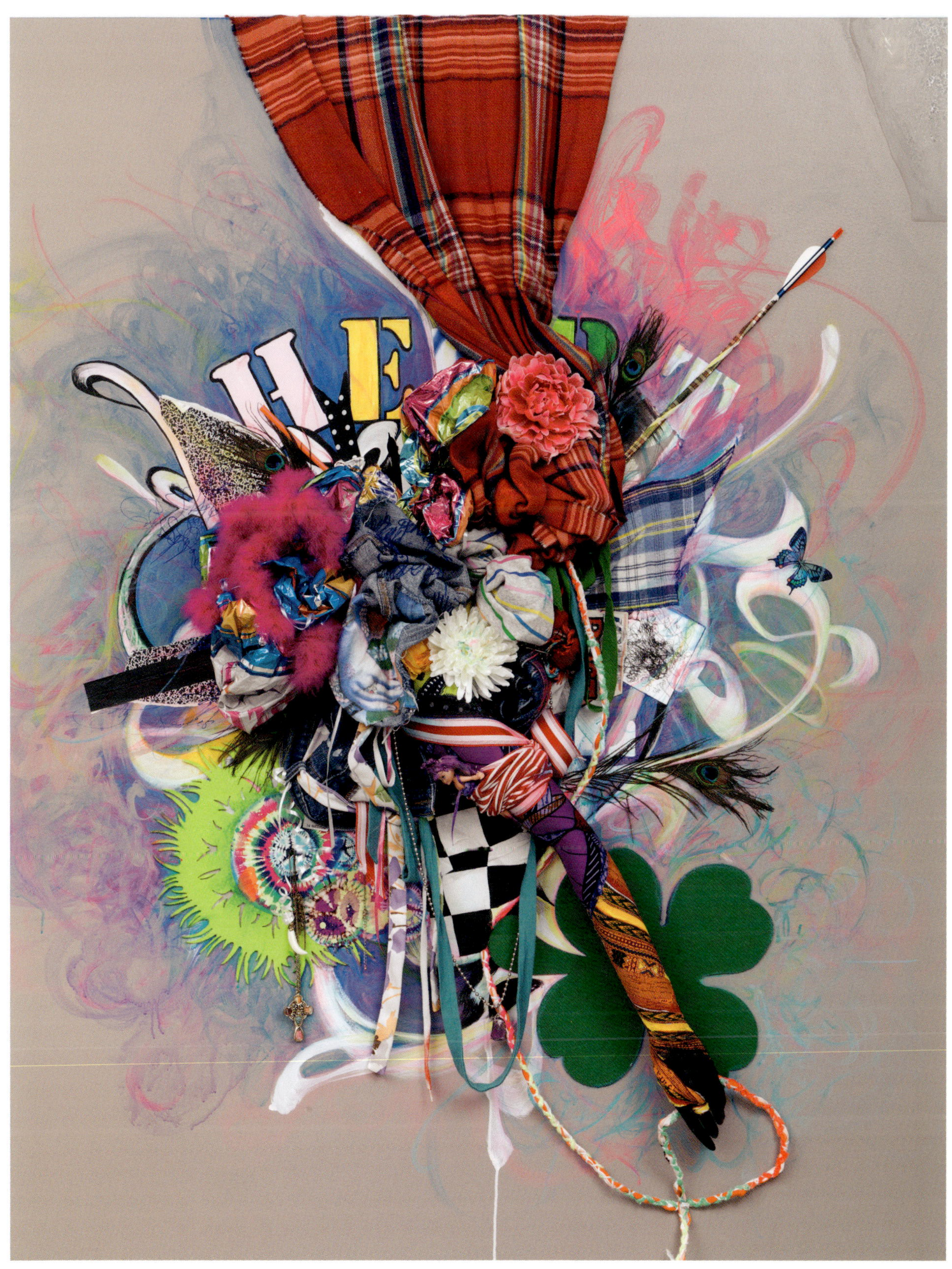

1   *Inner Clock*
    2014

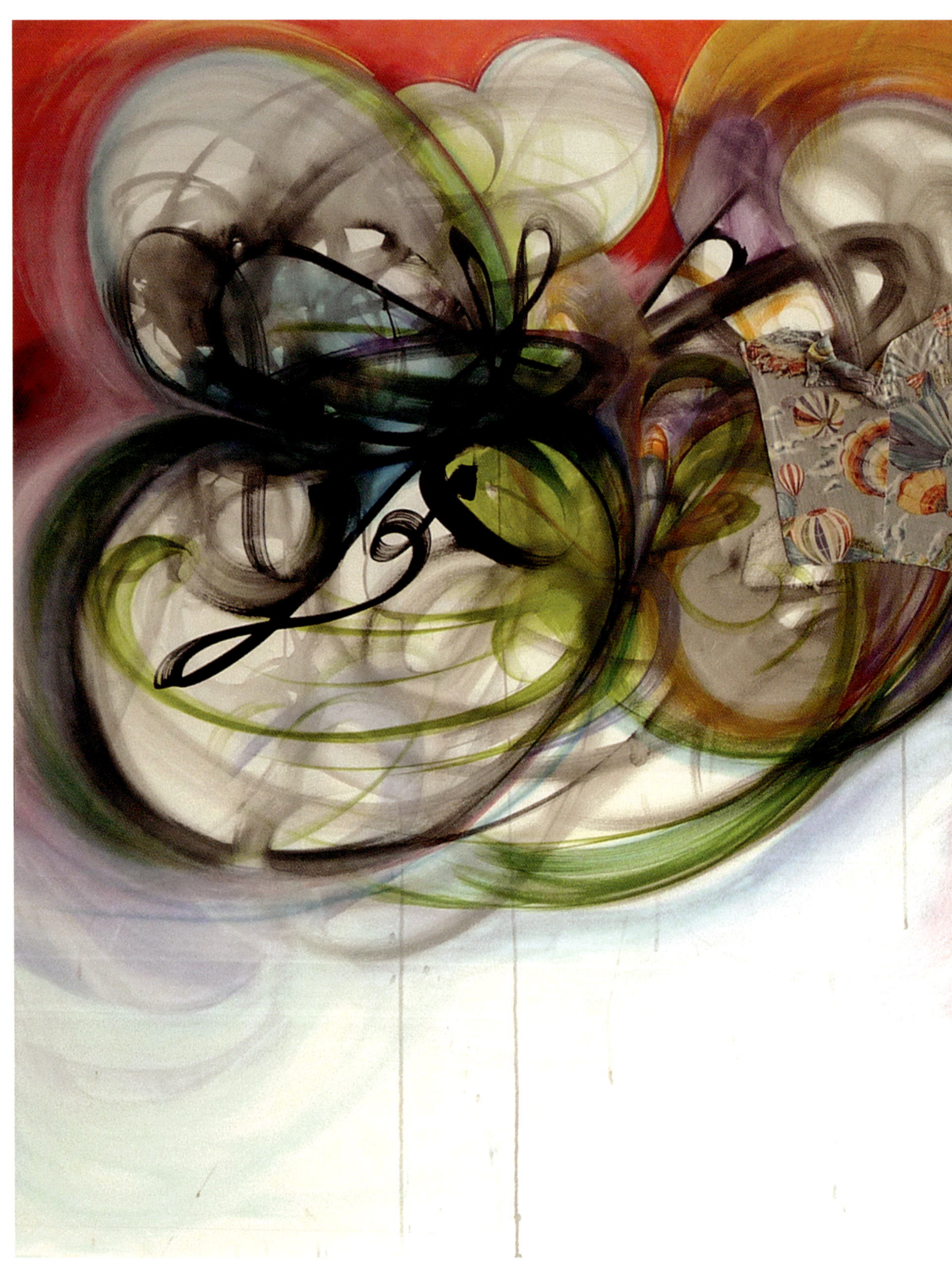

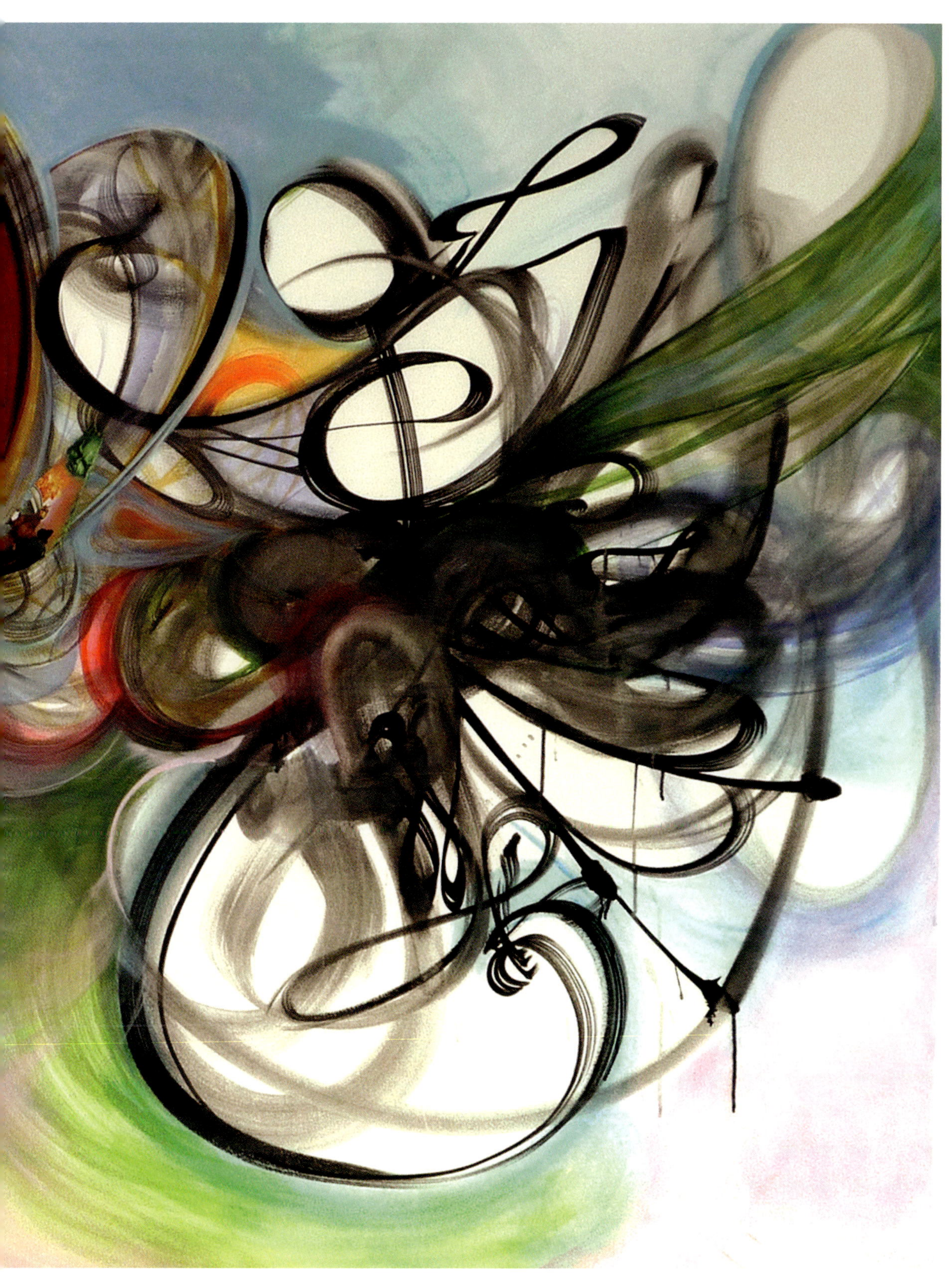

2   *Somewhere out there (in here)*
2011

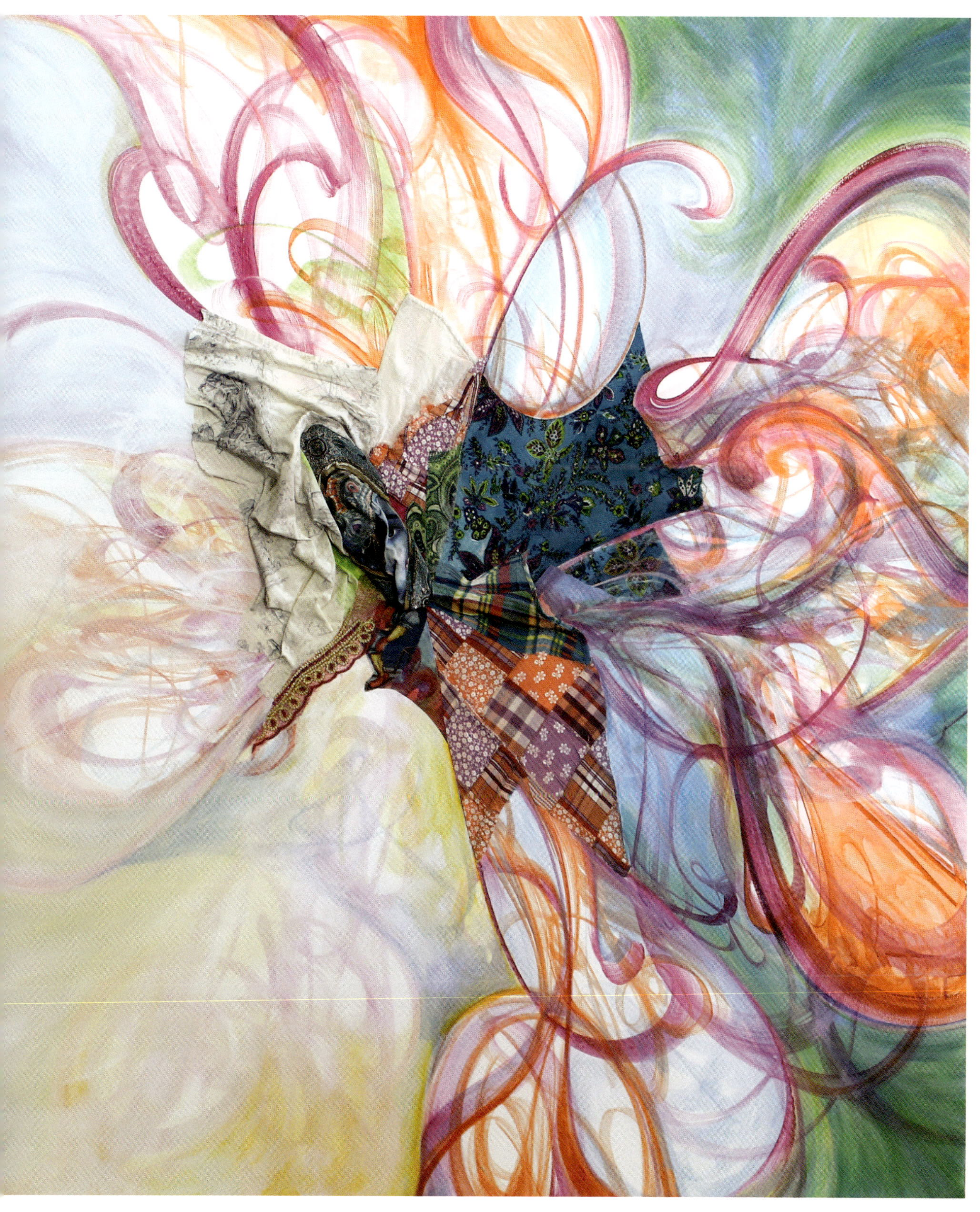

3   ***Tiny Dancer***
2013

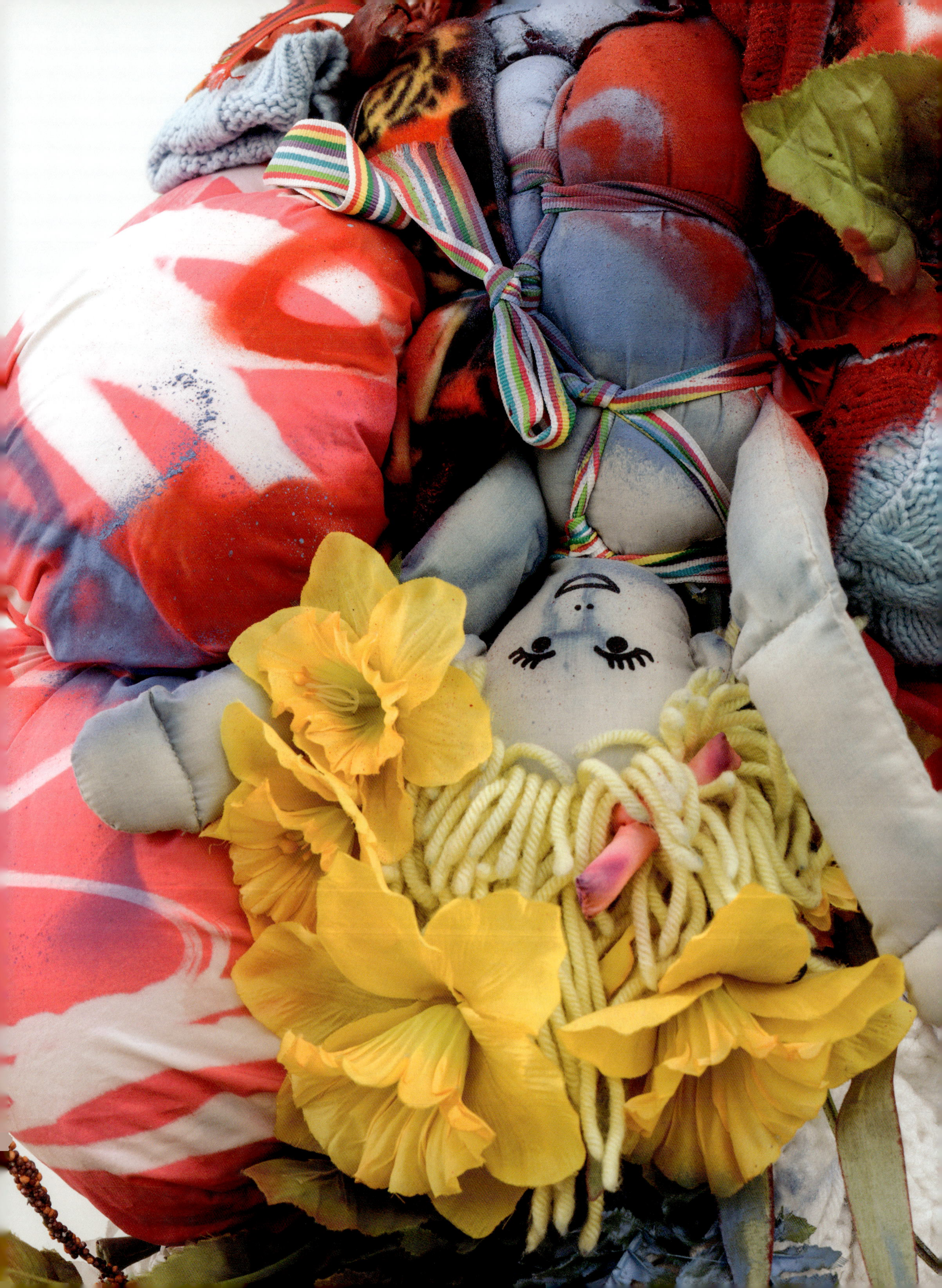

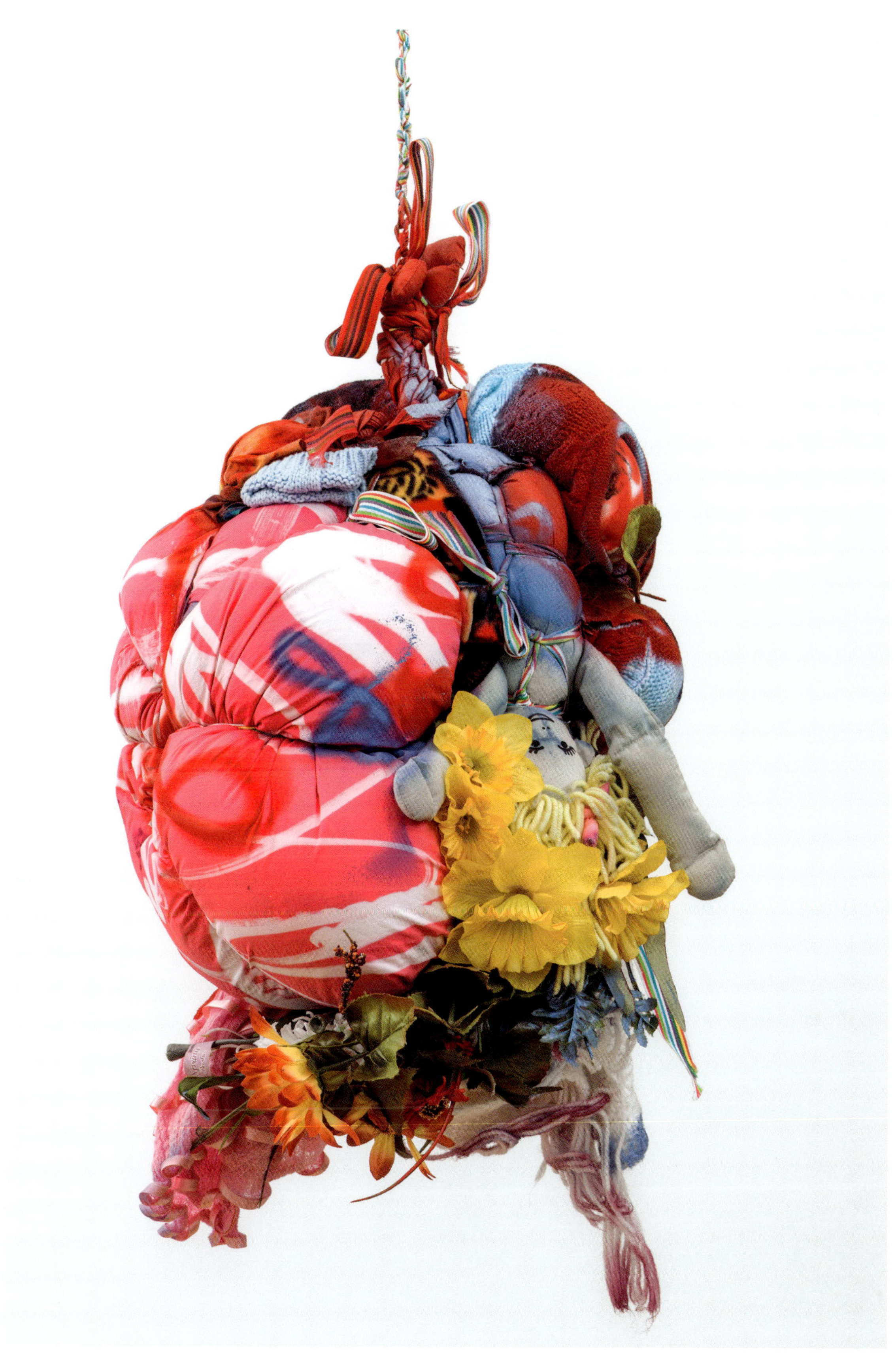

4   *Angel*
2011

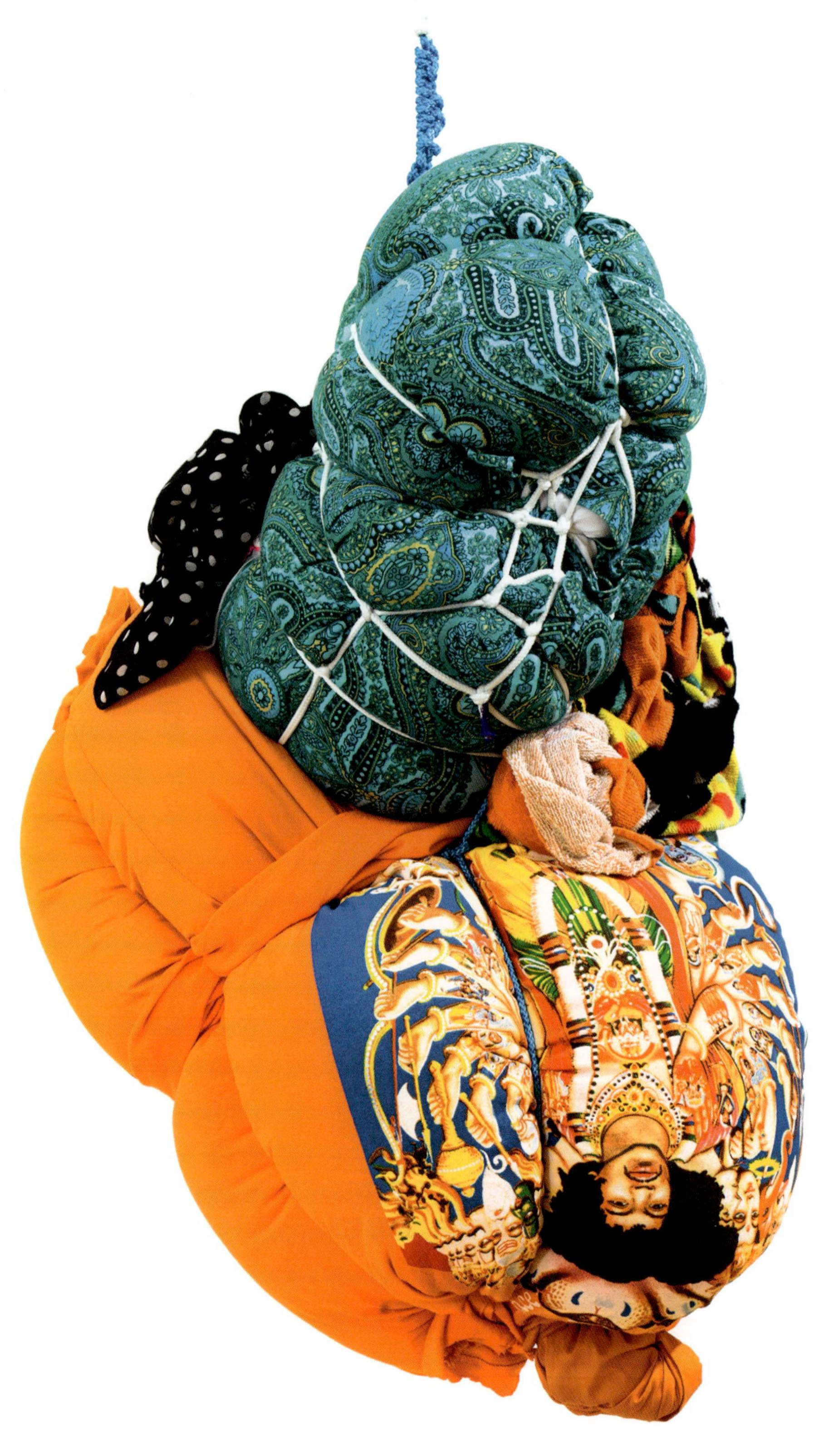

5 *Tongues became flowers*
2013

18

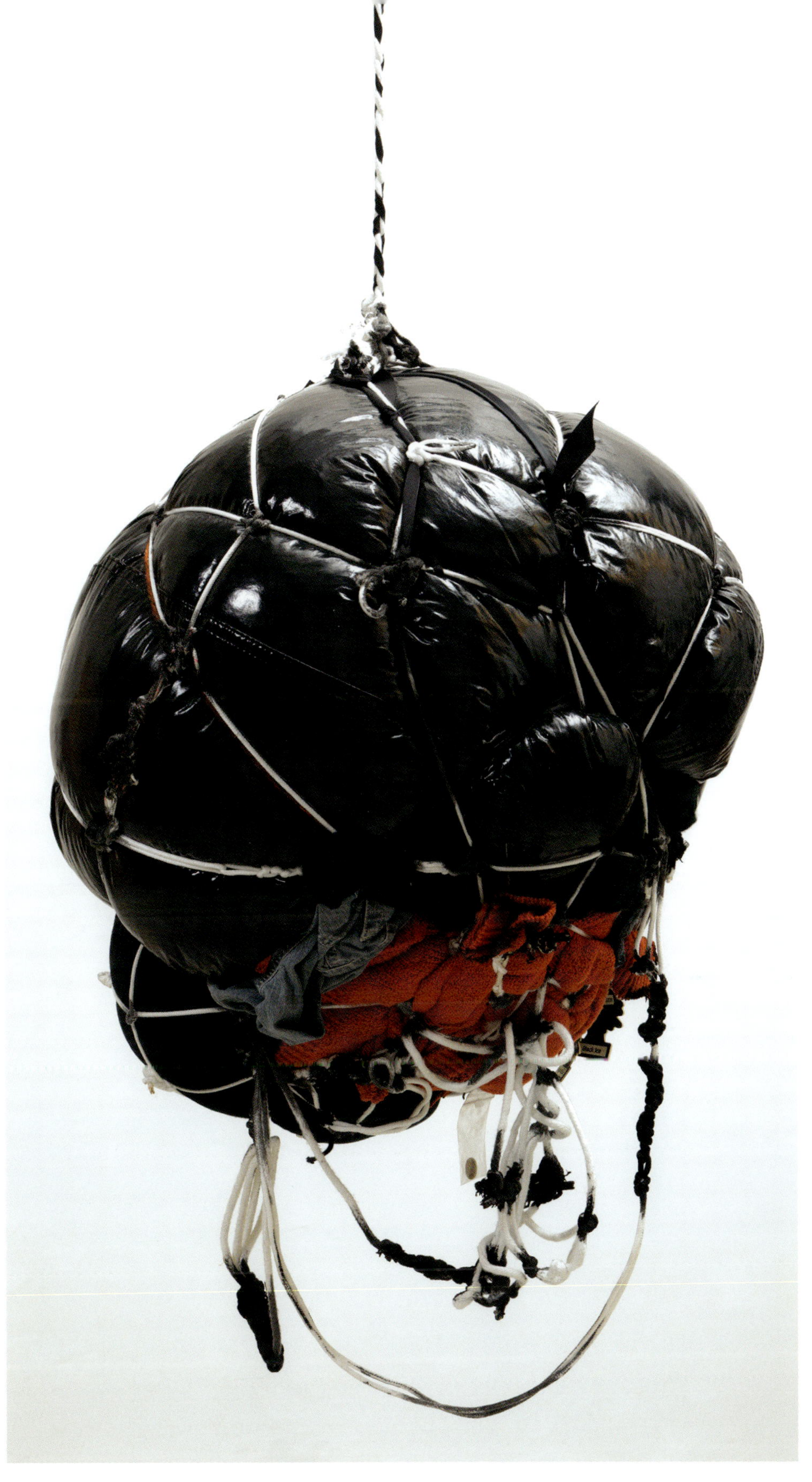

6   *Black Cluster*
2015

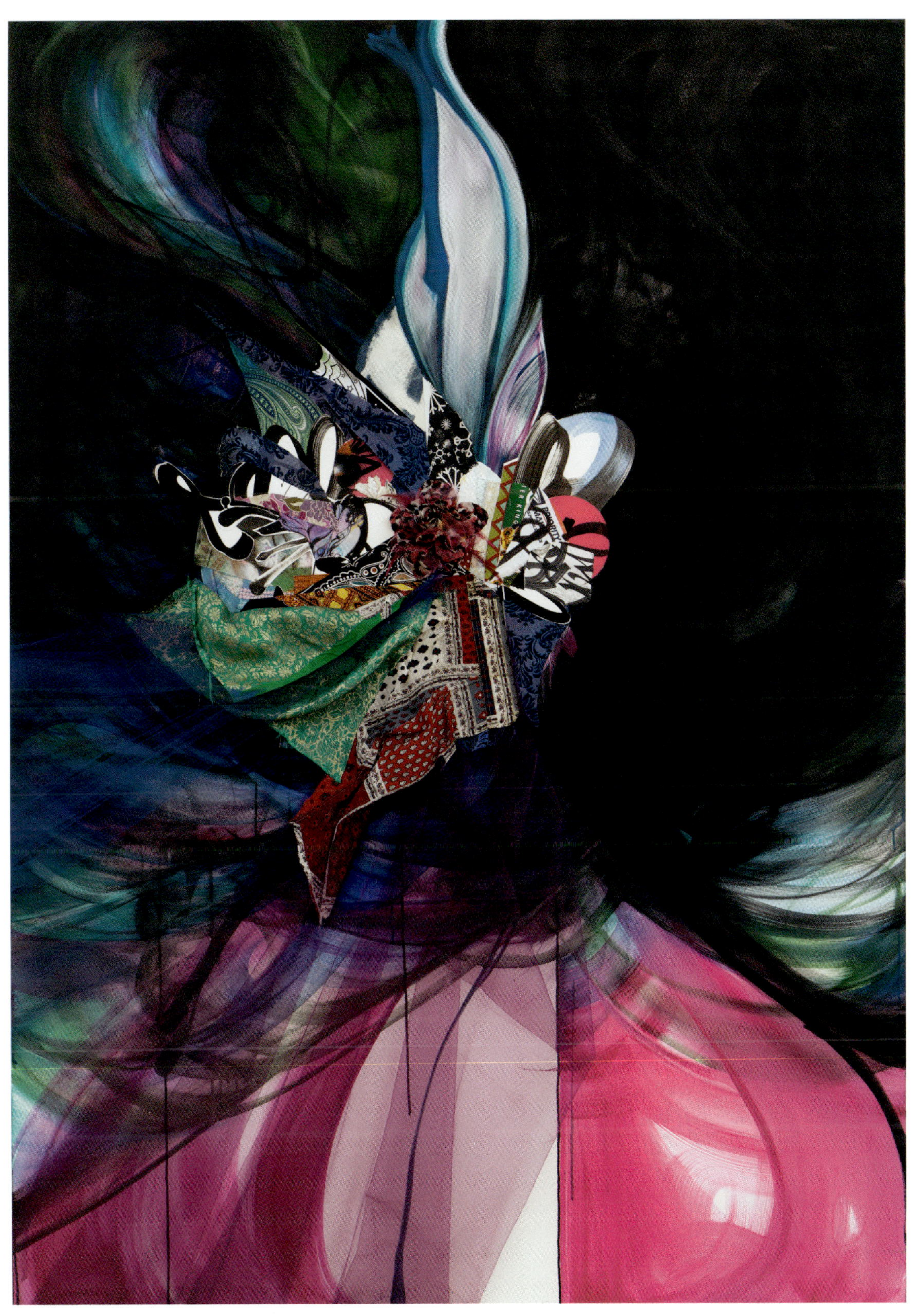

7 *When Shadows Fall (Home)*
2014

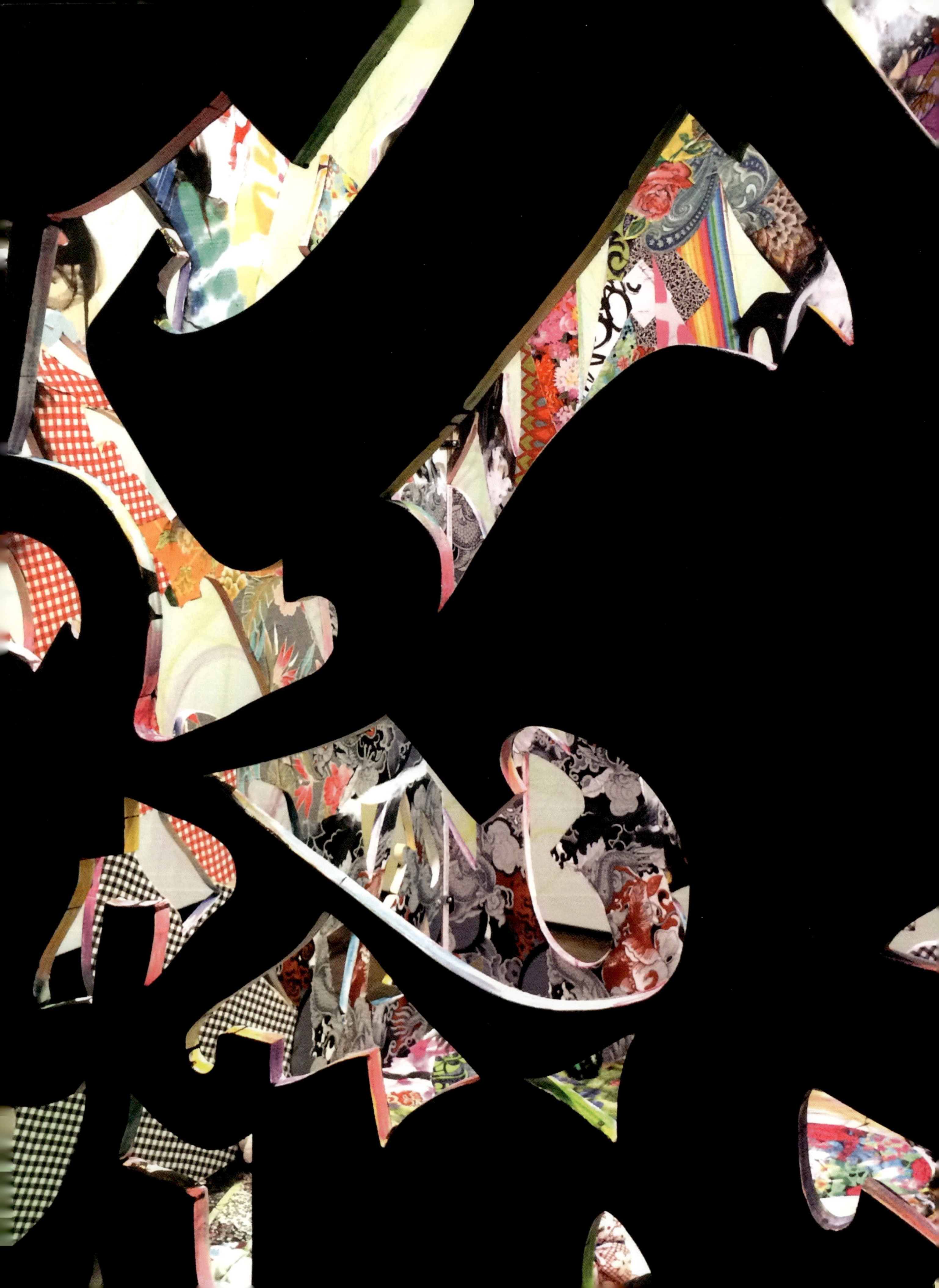

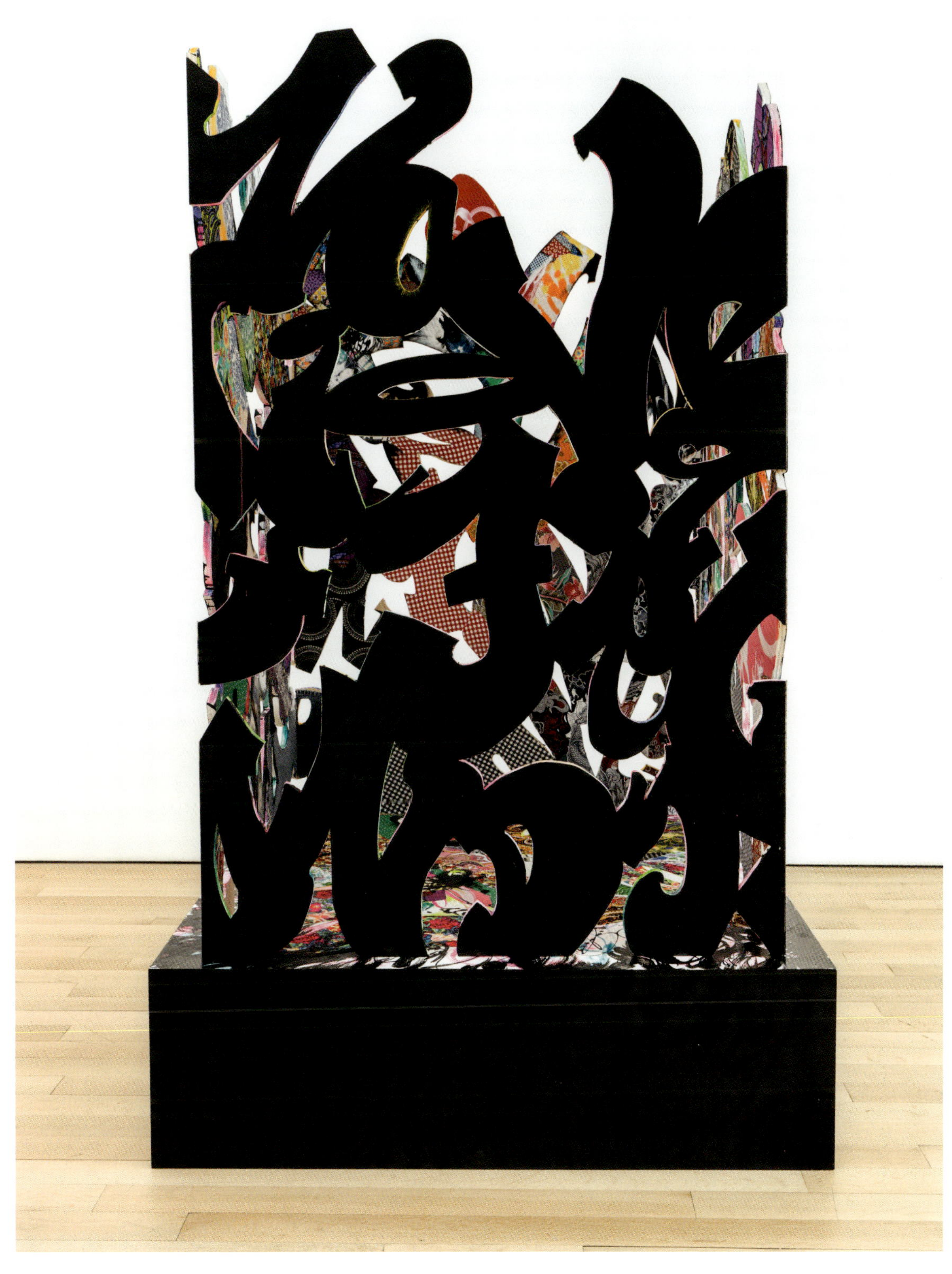

8   *Open Word Lattice (Black & Rainbow)*
2015

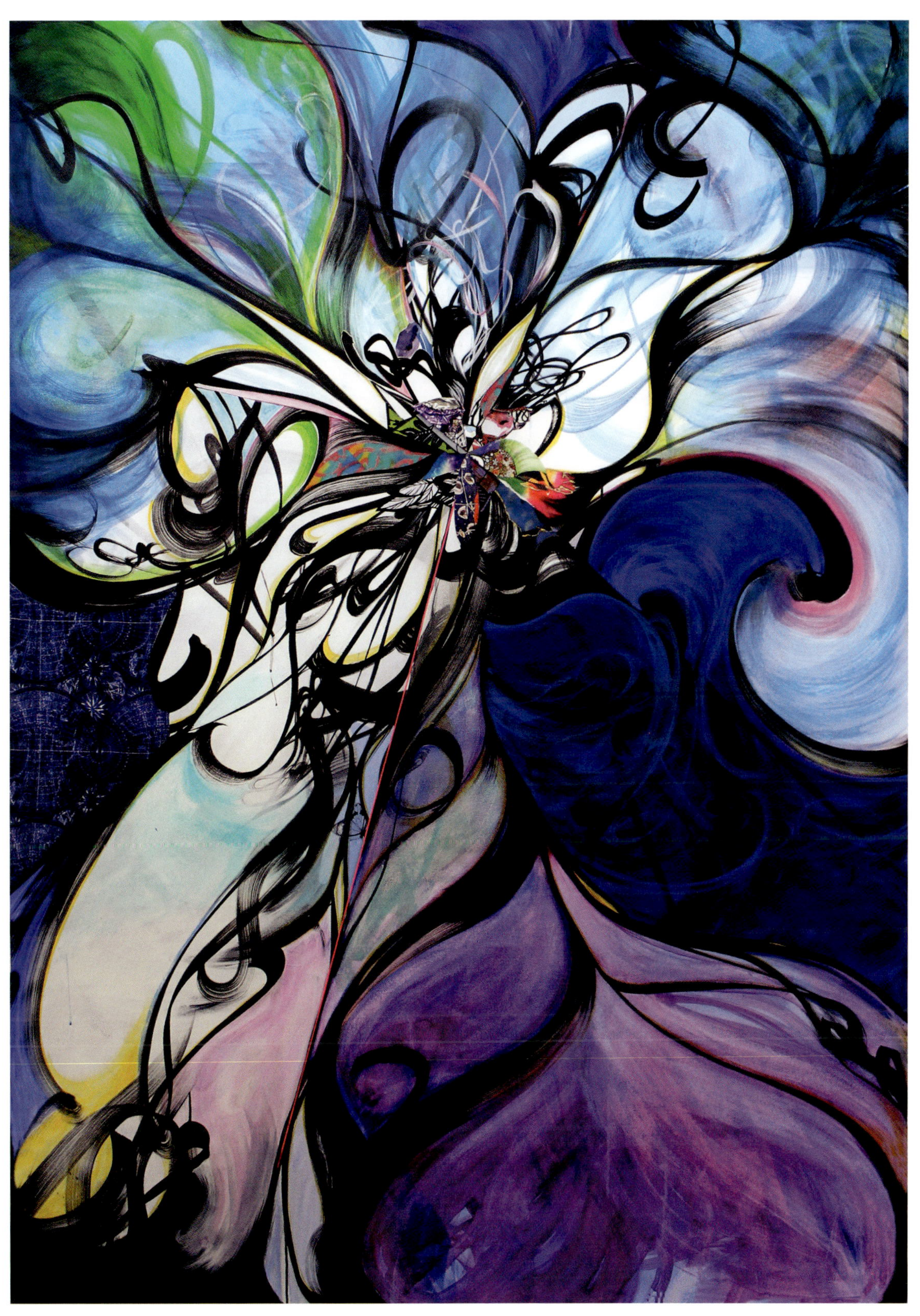

9 ***By the Light***
2013

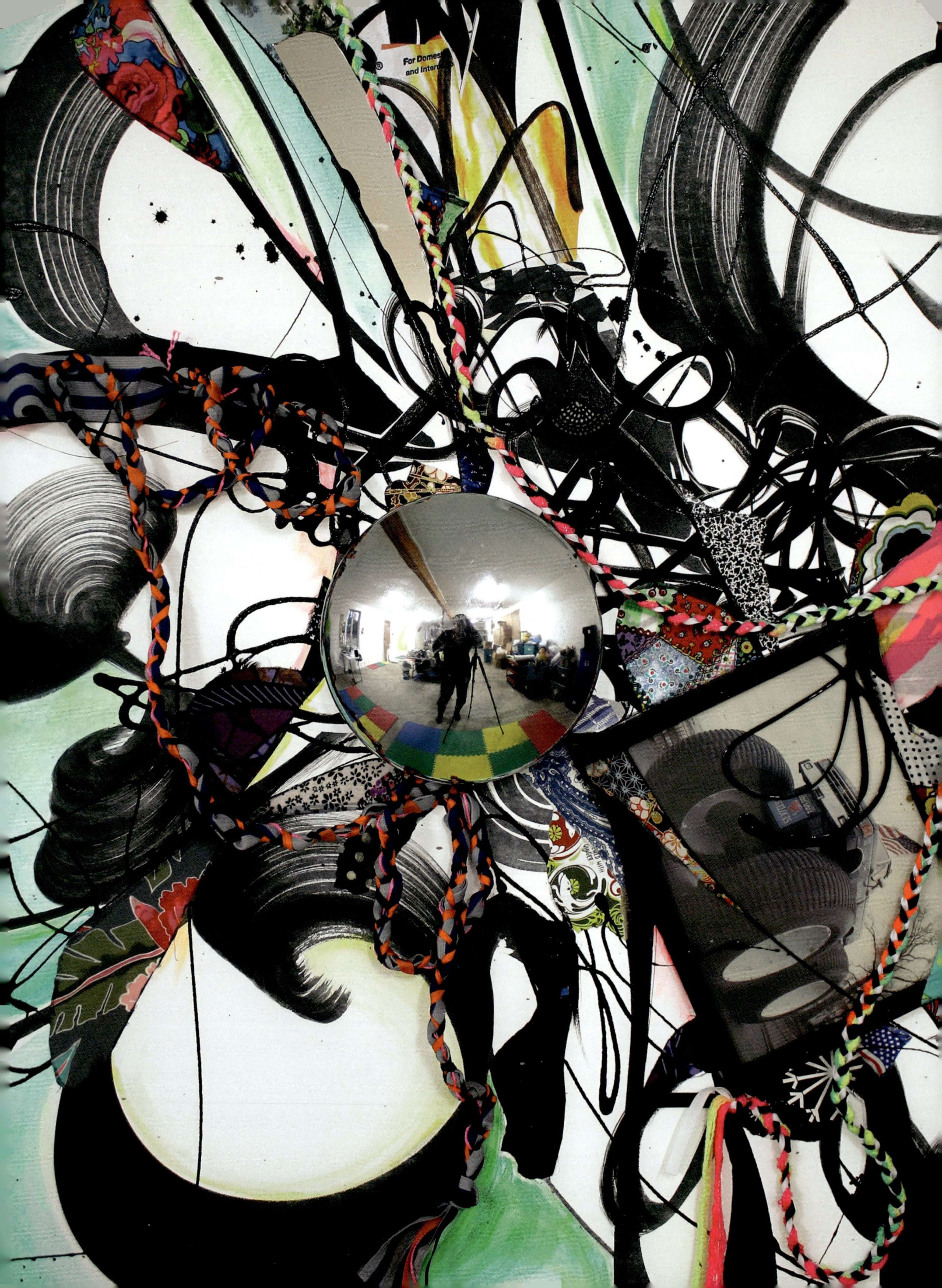

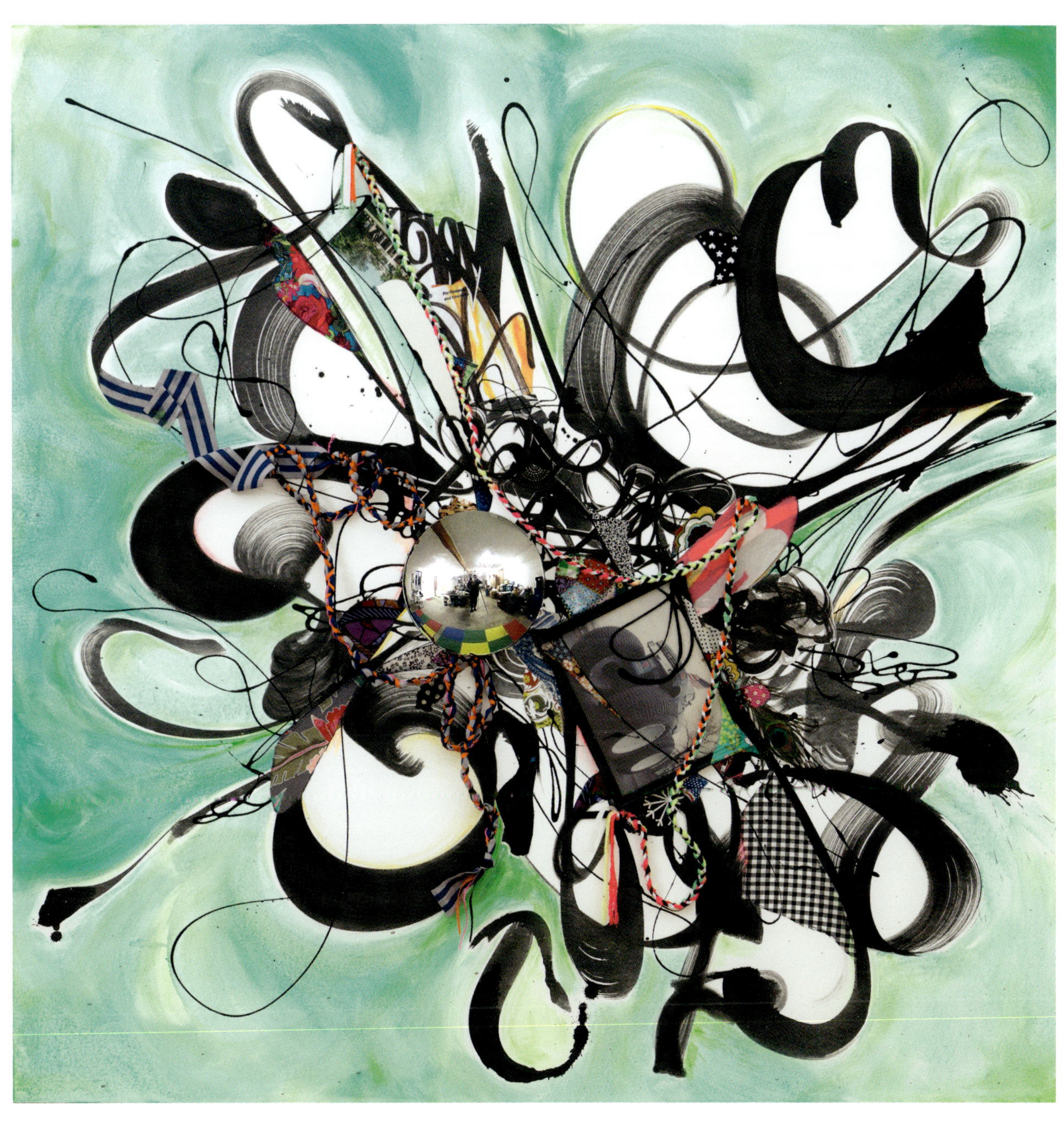

10   *Forever Strong*
2014

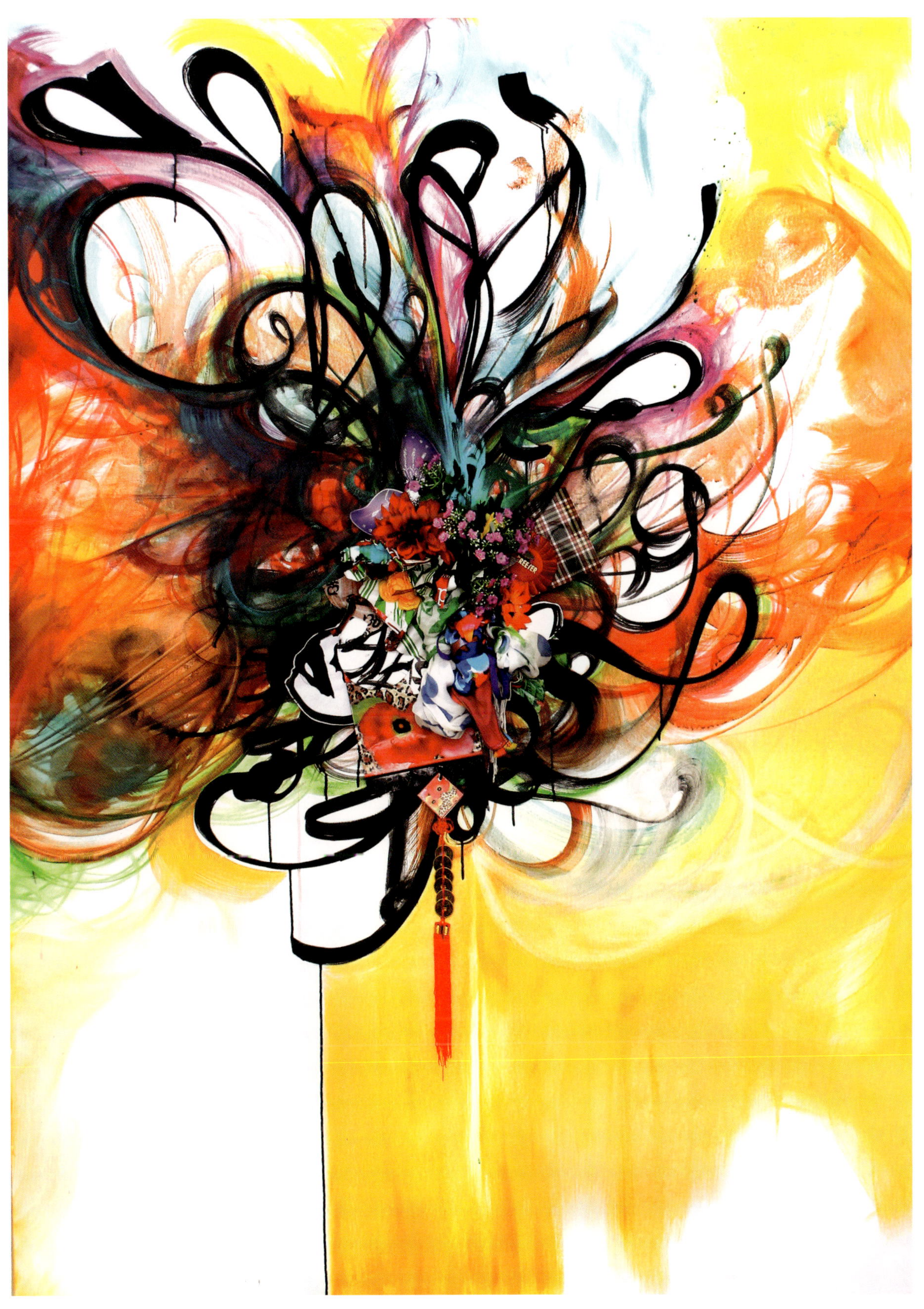

11   *Gifted*
2014

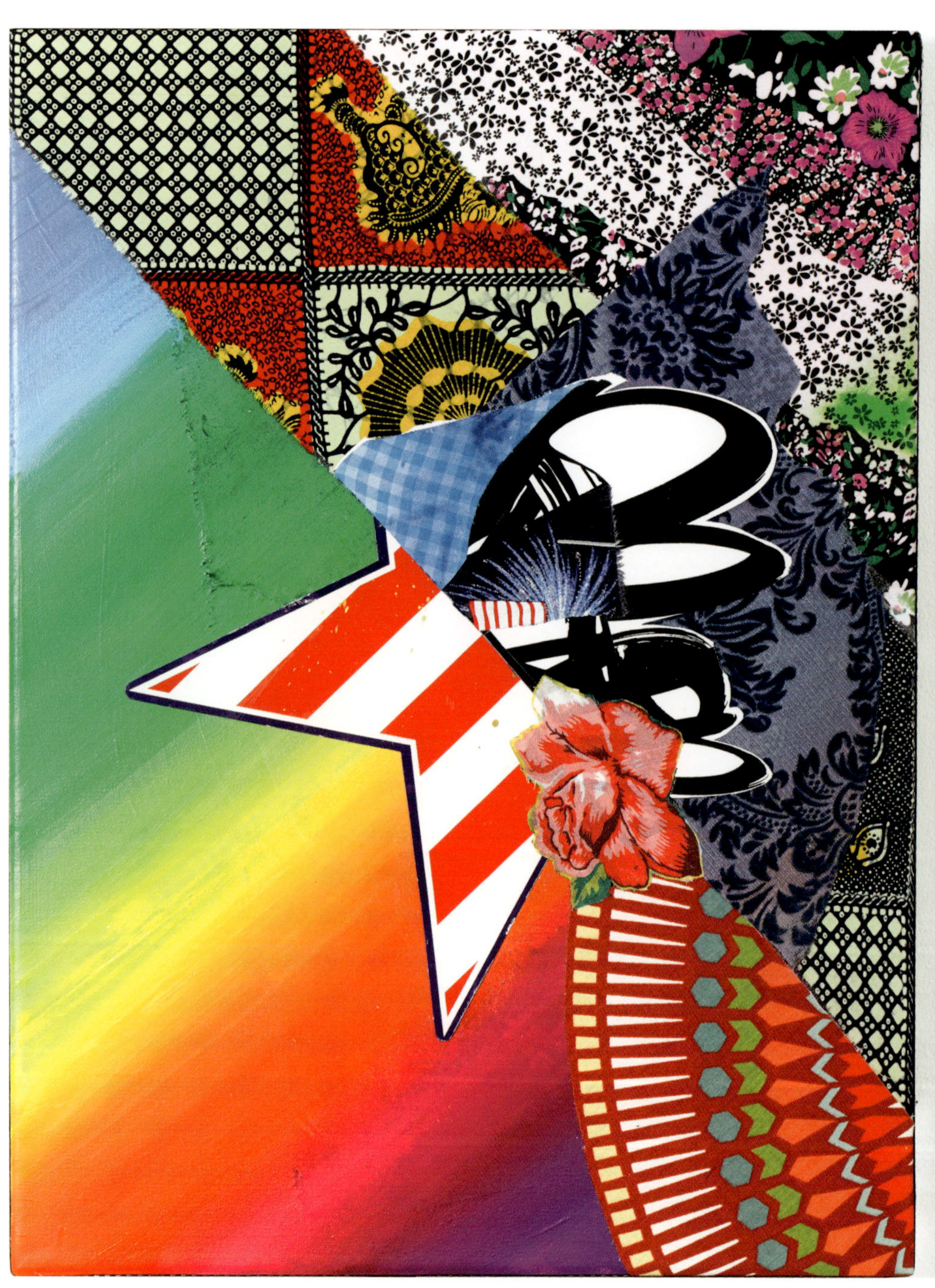

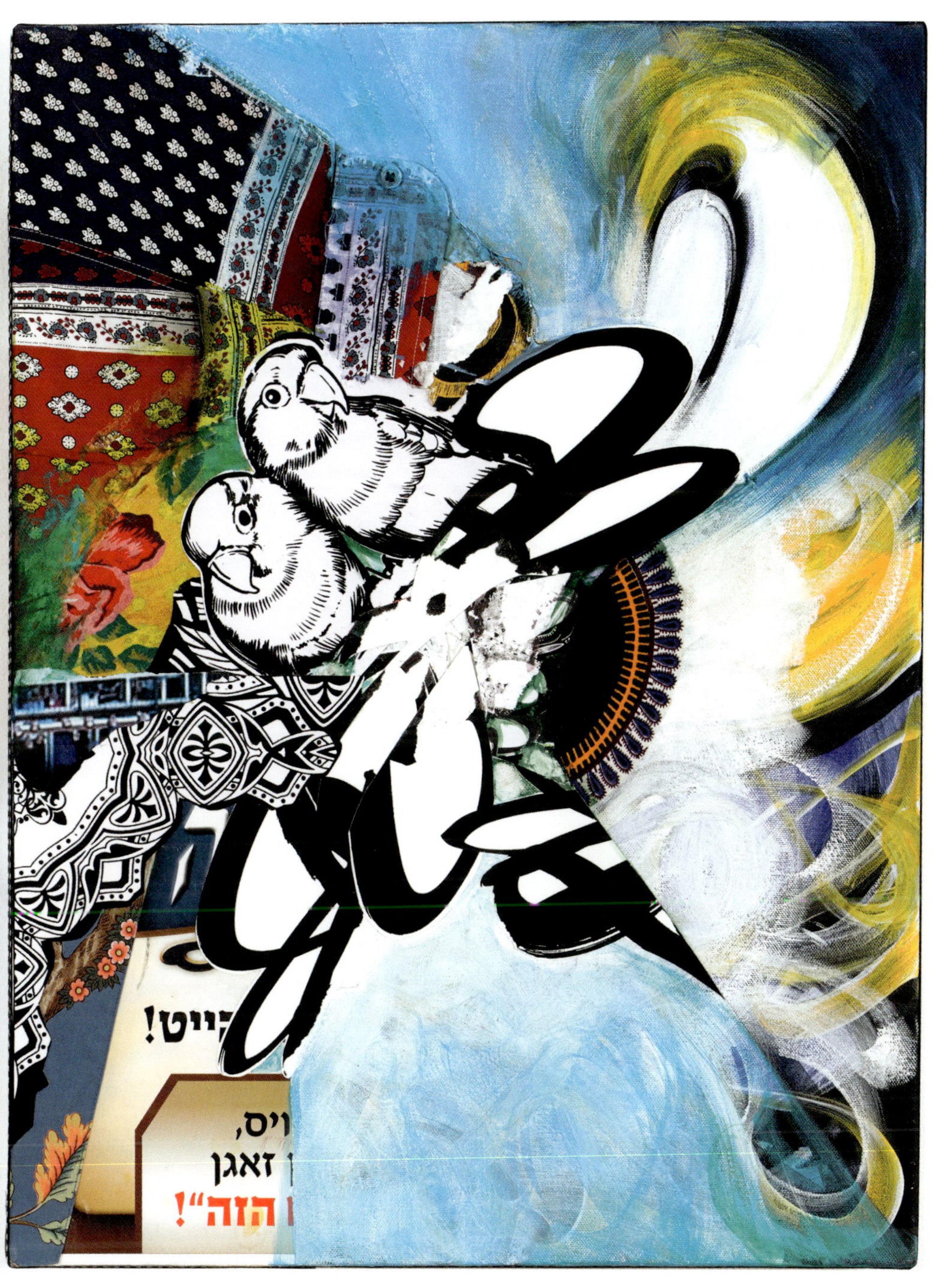

12   *Day/Night*
2011–13

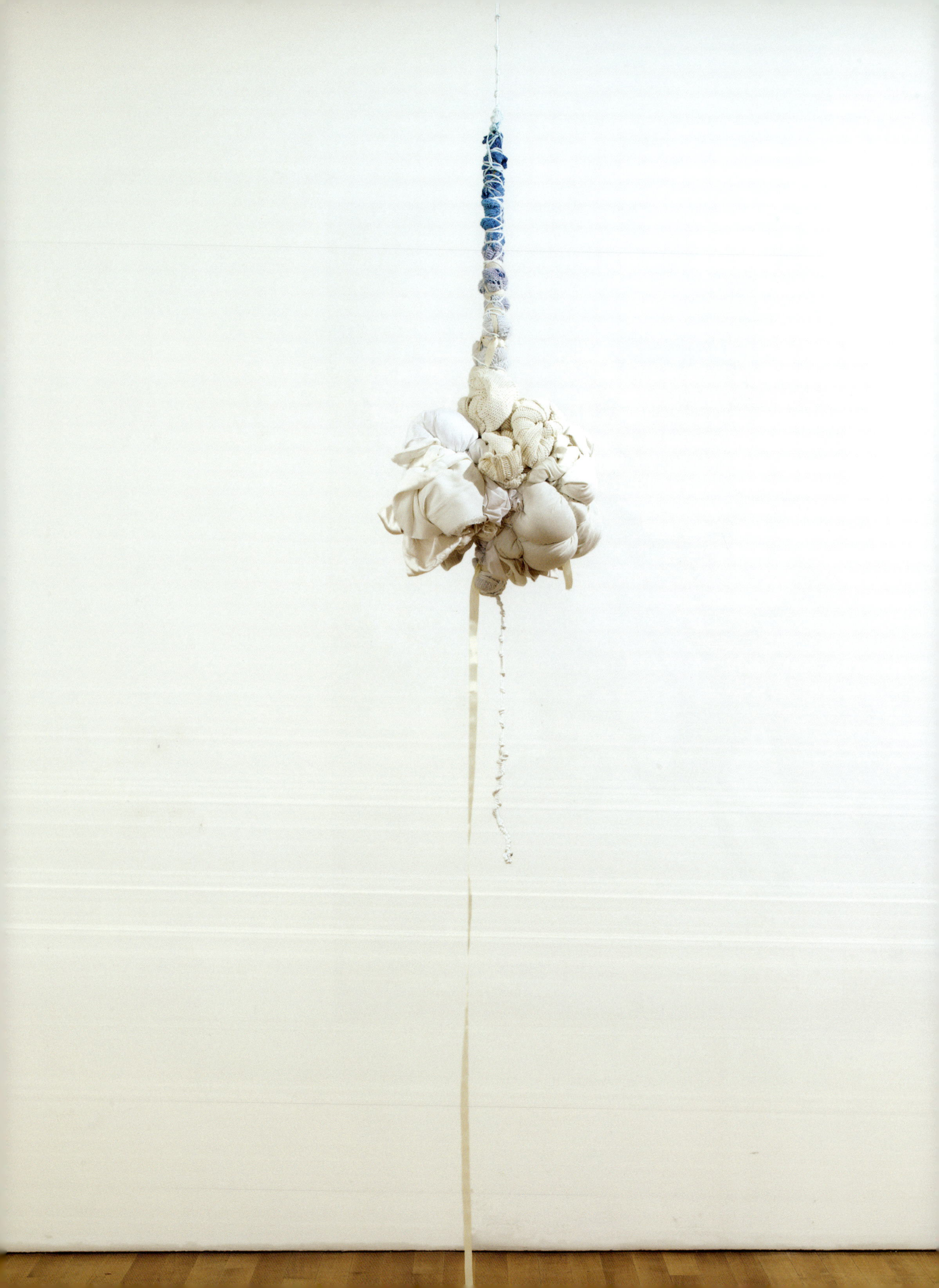

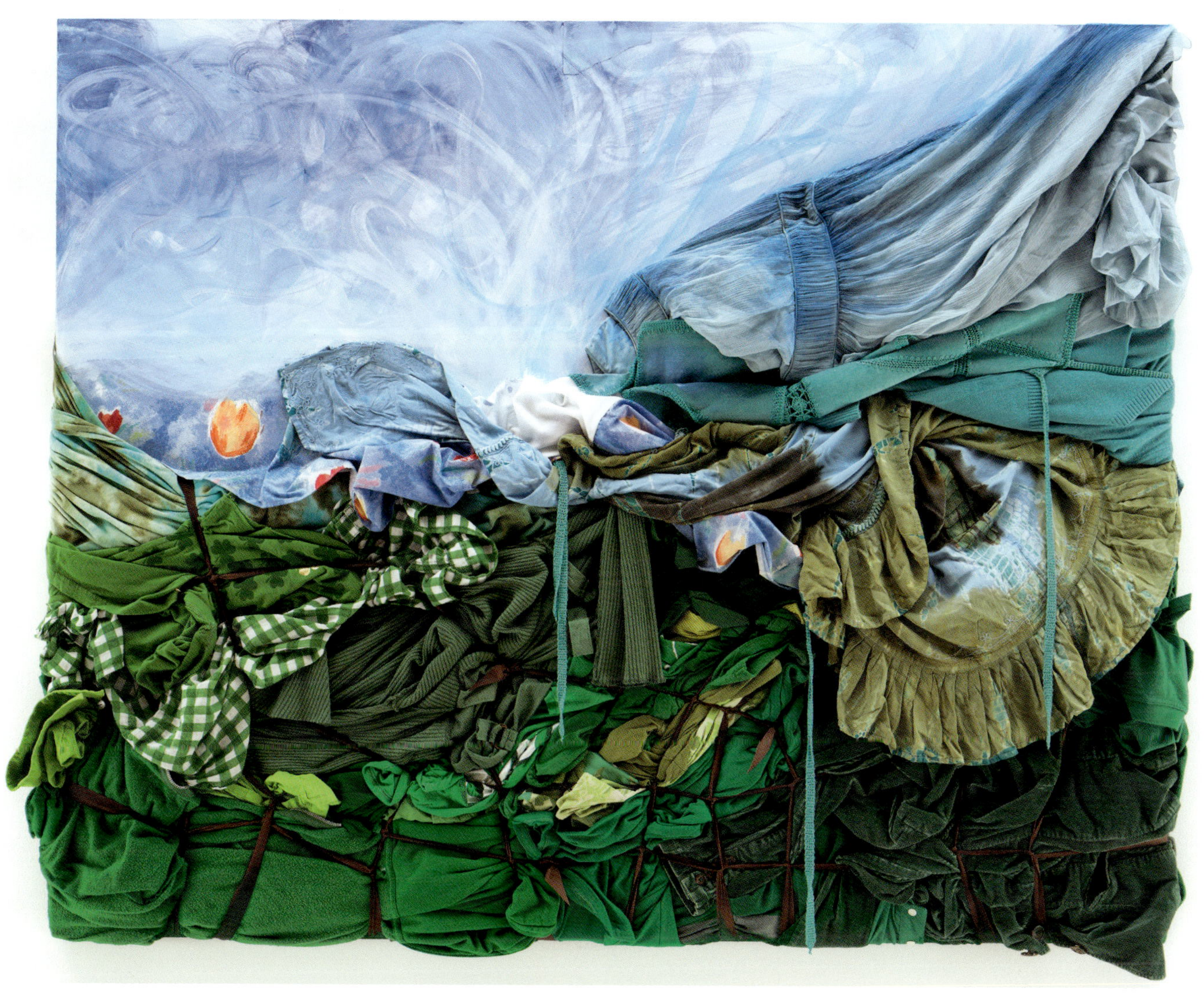

14   *Dusk*
2012

13   *Hammer*
2013

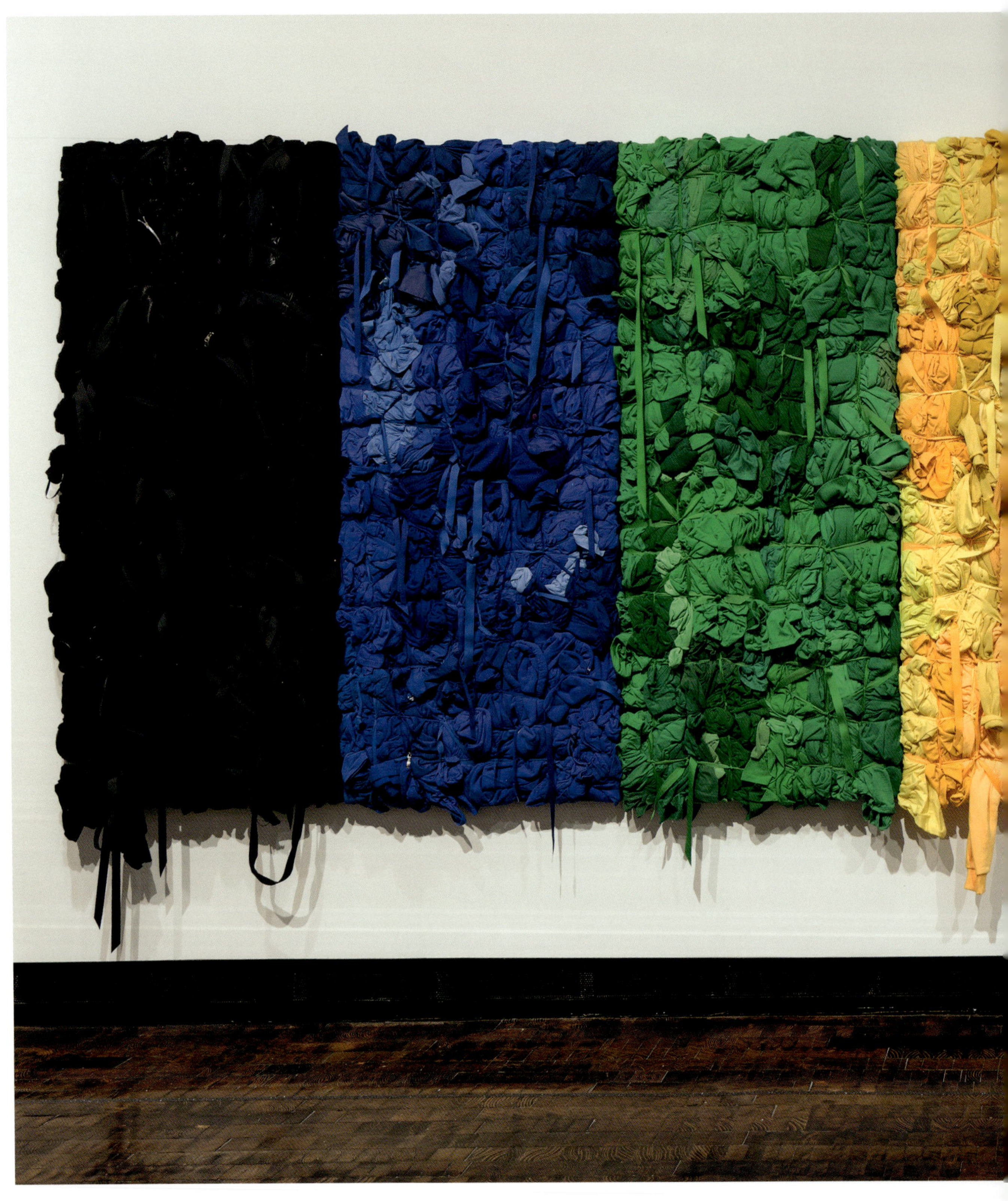

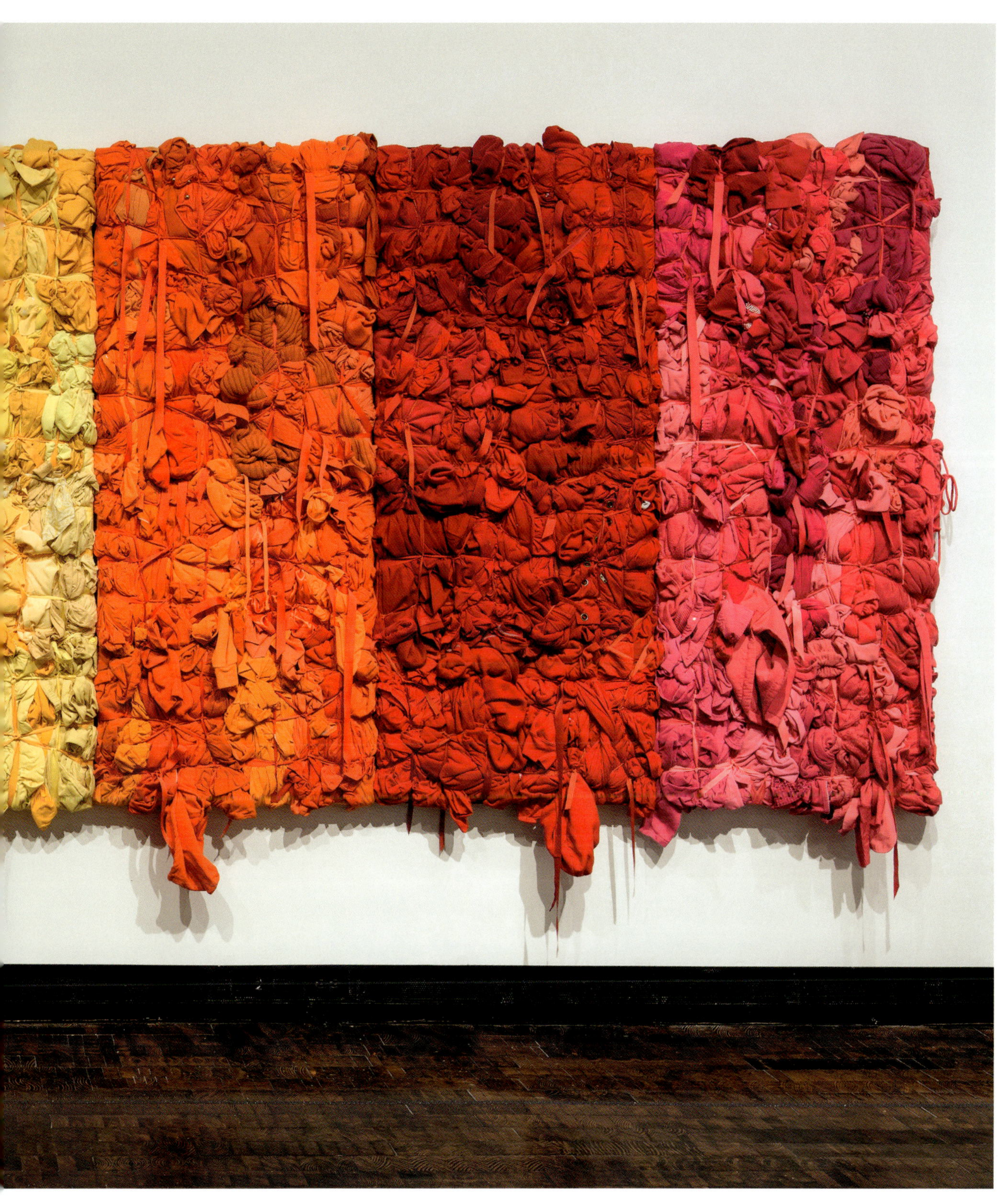

15   *Black/Blue/Green/Yellow/Orange/Red/Pink*
2015

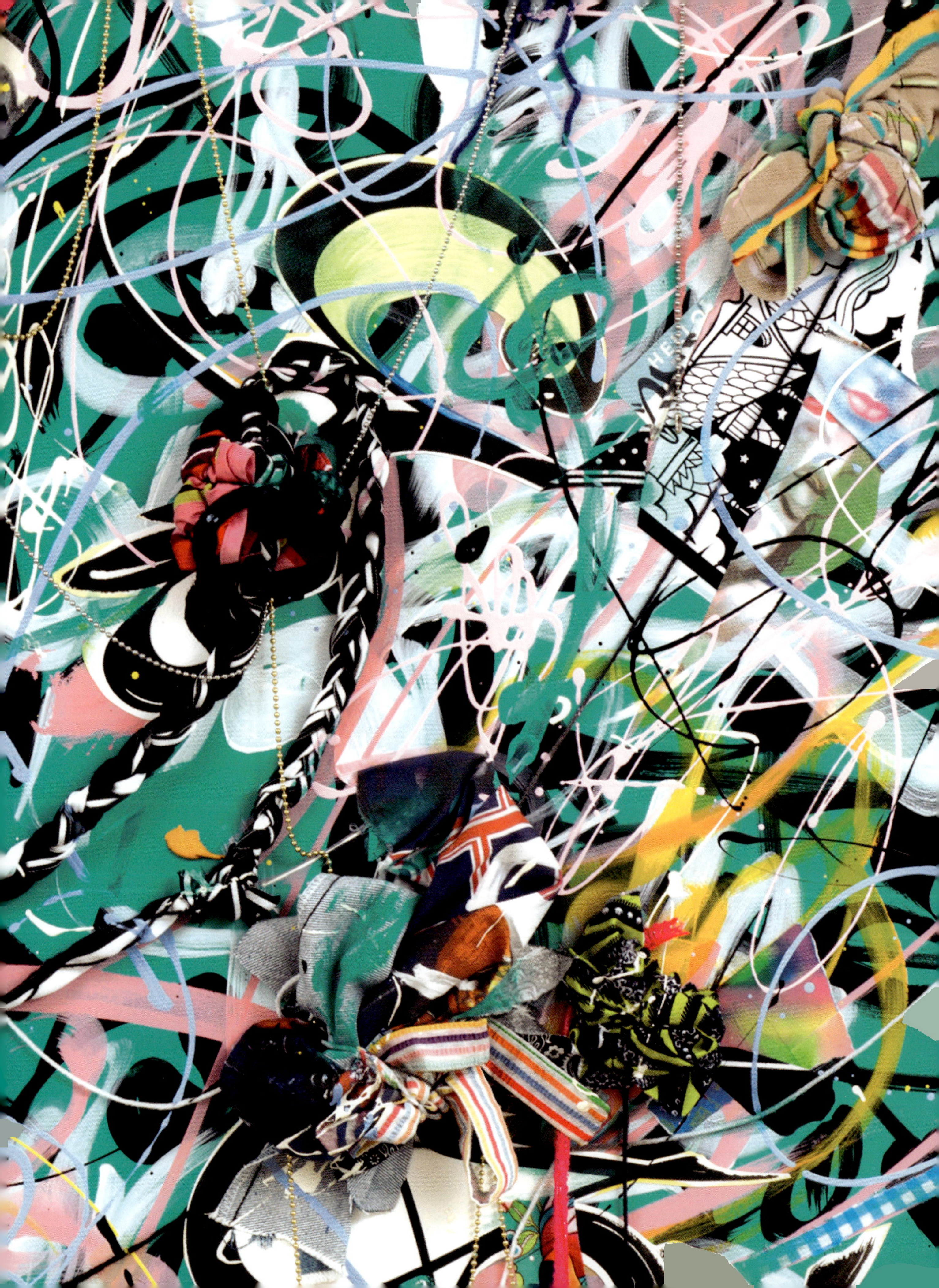

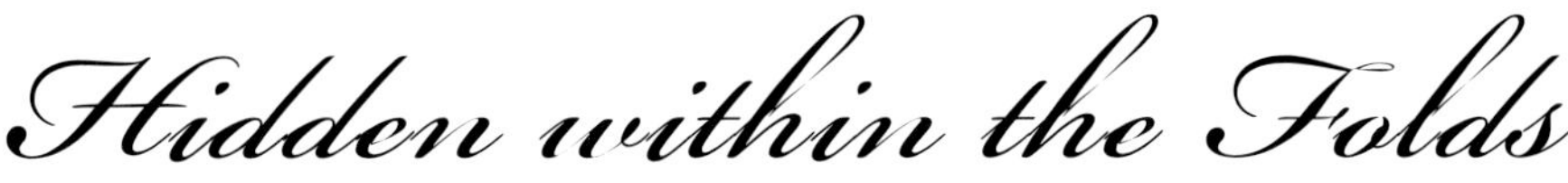

Hidden within the Folds

A Conversation with Shinique Smith

Jen Mergel

Robert L. Beal, Enid L. Beal and Bruce A. Beal Senior Curator of Contemporary Art
Museum of Fine Arts, Boston

Jen Mergel: While much attention has been paid to the tangible materiality of your work, I think its significant power lies in how it also evokes a specific atmosphere: of light, energy, memory and emotion. If dense materiality and open atmosphere seem like opposite ends of a spectrum, your work bends and bows that spectrum, bringing the ends closer together.

So let's start off by talking about rainbows. And wonder. Can you list what immediately comes to mind with the word "rainbow"?

Shinique Smith:
Oz
Dorothy
Wishes
what's at the end
On the other side
dark side of the moon
Bifrost
Rainbow Bridge
to a rainbow like you
Bows and flows of angel hair
the dizzy dancing way I feel
Redon paintings
Alma Thomas circular rainbow paintings
John McCracken Mandala rainbows
several old paintings with a landscape and rainbow

Niki de Saint Phalle
Air Supply
Put a Rainbow in the Sky
Cotton Candy on a Rainy Day
She's a Rainbow
I've got the world on a string
after the storm
storm chaser
i can see clearly now the rain is gone
i am a rainbow

JM: This is quite a stack of ideas, visions, and memories. It is packed with a wide range of allusions, much like your clustered columnar sculptures, the Bales. And it reminds me of one painting in particular. Let's talk about *Bright Matter* (plate 16). When I first looked at the colorful crunch of fabrics, the piece suggested the security of a childhood bedroom, surrounded by one's favorite soft things. But, with the black paint brushed on in areas, it also evokes a dense storm cloud, heavy and ready to burst.

SS: I like your description of the weight of the bundled clothing and fabric in the piece. It was not intentional to make it appear as a storm cloud, but indeed it does. Sometimes, things happen intuitively—in this case, the clarity of space happening where the rainbow is.

JM: This yin/yang of density with clarity seems essential to your work. It may be intuitive but it is also formally sophisticated, the conjunction of opacity with transparency, darkness with light. And it yields comparison to basic, yet profound, understandings of balance in life and creation. When we first discussed this painting in preparation for our 2014 exhibition at the Museum of Fine Arts, you talked about "bright matter" in opposition to the dense "dark matter" of the universe, and how ideas emerged beyond the material, to the metaphysical.

SS: When I titled this piece, I was thinking of the material, its color and its "seen" and physical presence, as bright matter. Then, I contemplated this further: Matter as a concern, as a problem to be solved through brightness or illumination.

JM: While astrophysicists may tackle matter as a problem to be solved, the way you tackle this lets us admire the beauty of the paradox. With your work, forces of matter and light, black holes and energy, can be approached through metaphor and visual sensation. Can you talk about the ideas of lightness and darkness in your work?

SS: Metaphorically, light and dark go hand in hand with gravity and weightlessness, with joy and pain. One understands more of one by experiencing the other. Our existence comprises dualisms that cannot exist without each other. I suppose that there are many ways to define light and dark, universally and personally. I cull my emotions and thoughts around both and find a balance or epiphany in the end, which I think comes from recognizing that they are the same, an illusion.

JM: This light-dark, joy-pain dualism is manifest visually in your work as well. You use light and dark not only as an idea, but a way to articulate imagery in space: shallow and deep, near and far, present and absent.

SS: My awareness of this came from basic drawing, from charcoal drawing, chiaroscuro and carving light out of grounded paper [i.e., by erasing parts of the paper's coating]. I approach aspects of my paintings this way.

JM: This way of sculpting light out of darkness makes me think of how you construct *When Shadows Fall (Home)* (plate 7). Along with the paint, you have employed transparency in fabrics, or alluring dimension through elements that hang. For me, these moments of veiled and layered imagery in your work belie romantic evocations of talismans and votive forms that beckon. In your words, what motivates these moves?

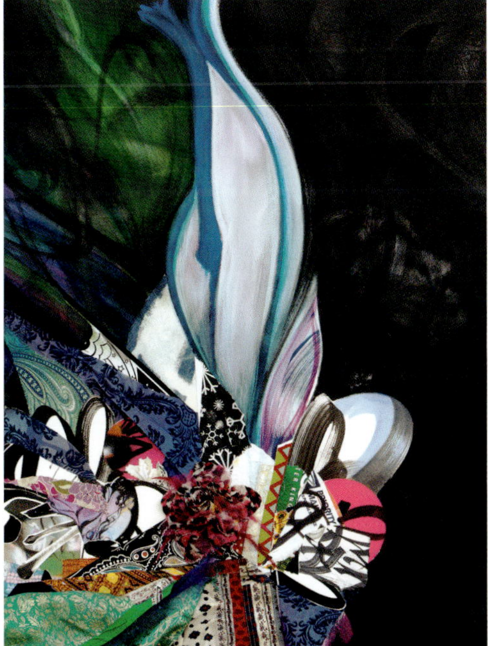

Fig. 1
Shinique Smith.
*When Shadows Fall
(Home)* (detail), 2014.
See plate 7.

SS: An attraction to bringing something from nothingness guided this piece. After starting in the studio, I stepped away from it to install an exhibition. While there, I was thinking of a friend, artist Terry Adkins, and our mutual appreciations for things. I had planned to call him when I got home, but on my return I learned he had passed away. I was confused and upset and, not knowing where to turn, went back into this piece. It began as a mostly pink and vibrant painting. Then Black infiltrated, and from the depths of this ground I began to carve a face with water. The colors from one of Terry's feathered sculptures kept popping into my head. Ultimately, a form hovering between becoming and disappearing became present in the work (figure 1). I signed the back "When Shadows Fall (Home) for Terry." The active looking, the mystery within the folds runs parallel to the aesthetic/formal capabilities of material and how layers of tulle can be layers of paint, color, and emotion.

JM: This is a strong example of seeing through something, peering in and discovering more. For me, it creates a magnetic pull of curiosity, of potential wonder to be sought. How and why do you employ that in your work? Can you talk about this in *Open Word Lattice (Black & Rainbow)* (plate 8)?

SS: I was thinking about inside out, fullness and lightness and the idea of an "infinity within." I want to be engaged as a viewer. I want to be an active viewer, to have layers and to look beyond the surface. I want to be able to read a work and to make associations to things outside the art world. I think my desire is to infuse my own work with details and considerations that create multiple reactions within my viewers. I don't want my work to be summed up with a glance. When there is mystery, I think it relates to the mystery of life hidden within the folds.

JM: And yet you also coil and wrap and implicitly hide elements from view in your bound sculptures, your paintings and even your performances. There are secrets stowed away that lure guessing. Perhaps surprise and discovery. Where does this instinct come from?

SS: I infuse my work with a sense of discovery, because that is what intrigues me and activates my imagination. It directly informs my process of making: I feel lured by the materials and elements that I use, yet do not know exactly how things will turn out. I allow myself to get lost and find my way back through the work. In this way I experience wonder and discovery and this transmits into the work's energy.

JM: What about wonder in self-discovery? In mining one's own past? Can you talk about *Inner Clock* (plate 1) in this context?

SS: In making *Inner Clock* I realized I was doing things I did in school, like highlighting things on my notebook and so I used those fluorescents. This led me to ballpoint pen–like doodling on my jeans and to composition notebooks. And the colors led to the illustrations in the book *KRSNA*, which I've had at home.[1] These associations and personal items began to form a transitional self-portrait that would become one of my favorite works.

JM: Transitional moments—child to teen, teen to adult, adult to aged, life to death—are often cathartic, poignant. You also layer allusions to such moments in your work. Can you talk about how and why?

SS: These moments are part of the objects and the life they had prior to my using them. And the relationships they recall or bring forward into the present become part of the work. I recognize and use them.

JM: Let's talk about the idea of the "sublime." In reading Anthony Doerr's 2014 novel *All the Light We Cannot See*, this definition of "sublimity" stood out for me: "It's the instant when one thing is about to become something else. Day to night, caterpillar to butterfly. Fawn to doe. Experiment to result. Boy to man." Like solid ice to gaseous mist, it's about transformation. Boy to man, girl to woman. What do you think of this idea in relation to the "sublime"?

SS: I could see this as part of the idea but not the absolute of it. Viewing a landscape like the Grand Canyon without overt transformation occurring could elicit a sublime experience. This may not be evoked by witnessing a physical transformation, but by seeing the product of one or because the experience produces a hybrid of meanings and associations, which could be particular to the individual. For example, on a recent train ride, somewhere between Rhinebeck and Manhattan we were delayed and I was reading for the first 10 minutes we were stopped. When I looked up, I saw a surprisingly strikingly beautiful landscape framed by the window like a picture. It was not unfamiliar—blue sky, green grass, nothing was moving or turning into another form. But the blue was truly blue and the green was very green tall grass

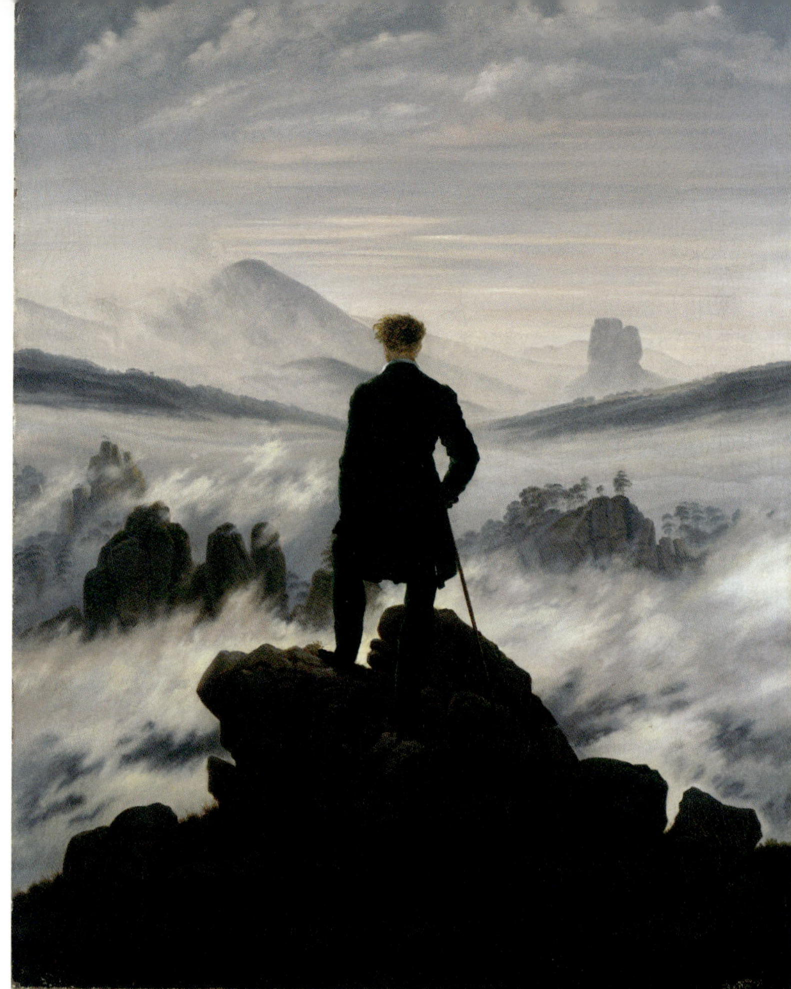

with wheat-like stems blowing in a breeze. The sun was filling everything. All at once I felt wonder at the sight of it and emotion at the associations of waves of grain and a mythic idea of America embedded in the scene. Is this also sublime?

JM: I think it's especially telling that you saw this scene framed by the window of a train as a perfect picture, instead of standing out on a mountain cliff. The classic reference of the Romantic sublime in art is Caspar David Friedrich's 1818 painting *Wanderer above the Sea of Fog* (figure 2). Here, the impression of Nature's infinite scale and power is overwhelming and terrifying to this lone onlooker as he watches something transform, perhaps ice to misty gas—the purest example of sublimity. I find it curious that the sublime in this respect is so safely distanced. I know the term's meaning was contested even when outlined by Edmund Burke in the 18th century, but by the 19th century, J. M. W. Turner's seascapes redefined the chill of a sunset marine drowning as a new sublime: violent, tragic, and enveloping. By modern times, the sublime became an absolute of the infinite and unknowable, not in nature but abstractions, like the *Black Square* of Kazimir Malevich. And now writers discuss the contemporary sublime in relationship to the mass scales of industrialization and information never before seen. While definitions have changed over centuries, they always relate to the ungraspable, the awe inspiring, something bigger than us. For you, what does "the sublime" mean?

SS: "The sublime" to me is the analytical construct that we've created to describe wonder. But analyzing events can inevitably suck all the wonder out of it—the analyzing creates distance from the truth of wonder that can only be gained by experience and which occurs within. The man in the painting is alone, in contemplation and reflection, in observation—he is aware not only of his landscape but of himself and his place in the world.

JM: Do you think the sublime could ever be internal, even intimate, if not "contained"? Like an energy?

SS: I would agree that being in awe of the vastness, a largess greater than us, is a sublime experience. But I think that there's a moment one can have within this when one feels no separation between the landscape or ocean or vastness. A momentary feeling of oneness: I feel this is the "sublimest" moment.

JM: What about the enveloping intensity, the implication of tragedy in the sublime in Turner's painting at the MFA, Boston (figure 3)? For me, it is arresting not only because it combines the glorious with the horrific, but also because of the balance between pure expressionist marks of intense color and utterly specific depiction. These tensions of sentiment and form are so extreme, they just barely resolve in the spatial logic of the scene. What do you think?

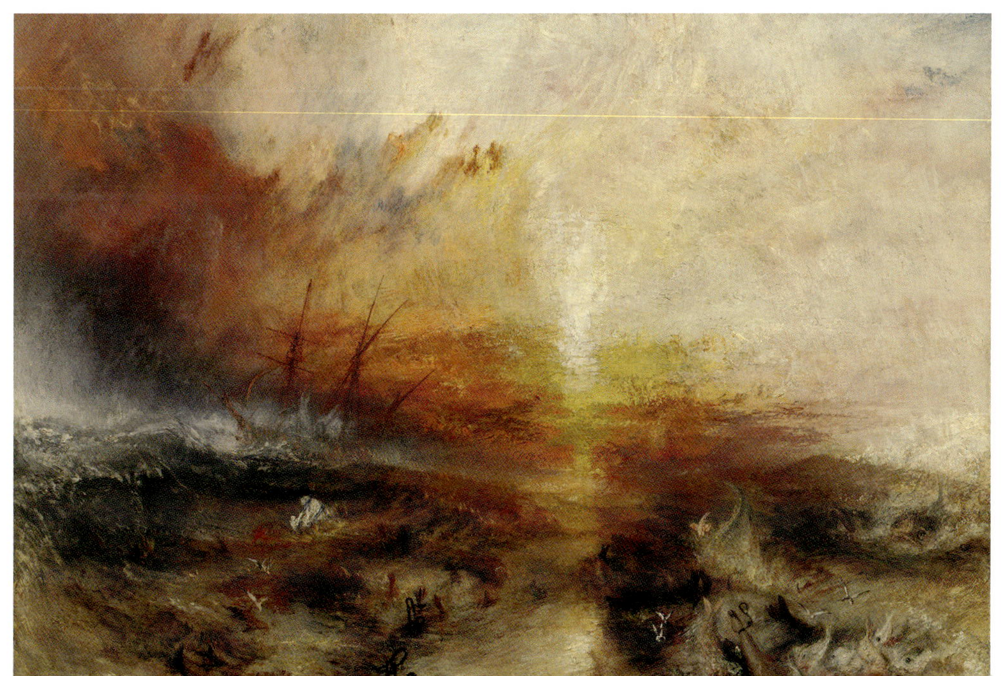

Fig. 3
Joseph Mallord William Turner (English, 1775–1851). *Slave Ship (Slavers Throwing Overboard the Dead and Dying, Typhoon Coming On)*, 1840. Oil on canvas. 35 3/4 x 48 1/4 in. Museum of Fine Arts, Boston, Henry Lillie Pierce Fund. Photograph © Museum of Fine Arts, Boston

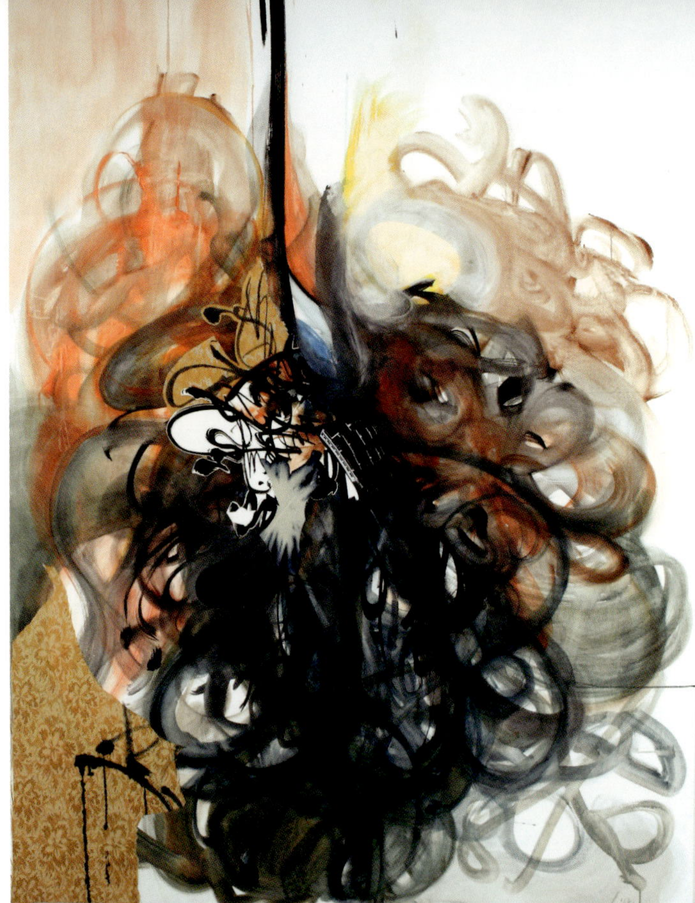

SS: The economy of content and gesture exudes a simple and clear power to me and reveals a refined, poetic and emotive hand. I think the changing values of light may have been an attraction, an intriguing exercise. And I feel that sense of wonder he may have viewed in every sunset he observed and painted.

I think that the best art absorbs, records and translates an honest experience to the viewer, and for me, as a practitioner, I am intrigued by the thought process in his works. *The Slave Ship* is different because of its content and, as you say, the glorious with the horrific. The beauty of the work outweighs what is transpiring and I find that disturbing and almost counterintuitive to his intent. Possibly this is what makes it eerie to us. I know there was a rainbow after this.

JM: Why the certainty about the rainbow? In this case, what could it mean?

SS: The rainbow, we still look for after a storm. We know why it is formed and it still inspires us, maybe because it is fresh and pure after a period of darkness.

JM: What is the difference for you between wonder and the sublime?

SS: Wonder is a natural human reaction and the sublime is a philosophical-analytical construction to explain this state. I think we all have different moments, things and situations that evoke this sense. Wonder is intimate. It is experience. The sublime is a greater reflection of how we perceive ourselves in this world, our relationship to life and ourselves.

JM: About wonder, there are at least two ways to think of it: one is "unspeaking awe" and the other is "verbalized curiosity," as in "I wonder where all of these scraps came from, who owned them, what were their past lives?" I think both types of wonder are powerful and energize responses that art can elicit. What are the ways you think of wonder?

SS: I see wonder as a feeling or condition and as an active curiosity too. Another example: We are surrounded by nature at my home, and there is a meadow that surprised us our first summer with being a natural habitat for fireflies. There can be hundreds of them, maybe a thousand or more. They prick the fuzzy darkness before us, and sparkle, and flash like an orchestrated light show. The longer you look the more hypnotic and deliberate the blinking patterns become. Along with this effervescent display, there are three types of frogs in a symphony in sync with the lights flashing. Their sounds are emphasized by the rhythms of the small points of light. There is a multitude before us. I had seen fireflies as a child; they were wondrous then. Though familiar, they are more wondrous as an adult.

JM: So wonder builds upon personal memory and connection to childhood?

SS: It is a deeper experience now because we remember our childhood experience: trying to catch those flashes, the smell of grass and the sultry summer air under the color of twilight. The classic romance of recalling youthful wonder fills us all as adults who can now synthesize feelings into an even more complex emotional state of wonder. It may remind us of not only a past time, but also who we were and how we perceived the world and everything around us with this sense of "wonderment." Importantly, it could also represent how we wish things in our youth could have been. Now, in the summer at my home, we are swayed by this rhythm and beauty every night. Perhaps, the feeling and the action go hand in hand, and the curiosity of how they glow or why they flash is part of it.

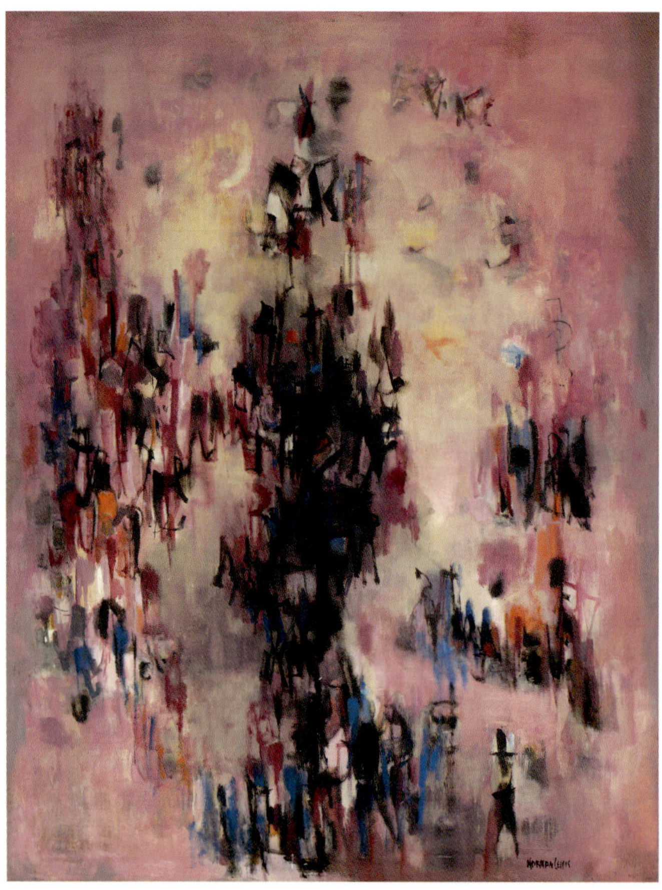

JM: Do you believe the atmospheric—mist, light, and natural rhythms of energy—have not just wonder, but power, in today's world?

SS: Yes, it always has and will as long as we breathe air and the sun shines.

JM: True. And in thinking about art, I have been considering how atmosphere and abstractions can have power. I was reading about Norman Lewis's atmospheric abstract "black" paintings made after the Harlem Renaissance and through the civil rights movement (figure 5). It is argued he used black as a color in its own right, not a secondary hue to tone or darken others or an opposite of white, but a dynamic pigment that could stand on its own. And his "ritual" paintings often hinted at gatherings or assemblies in an open-ended way. For me, the subtlety of the color shifts keeps me looking. You can see a shimmer of a "gathering incident" in just a few slightly differently toned and thickened marks. What do you think of Lewis's image? How would you describe the energy in it?

SS: I admire this work because it is spatial to me. I am not of the same era, when congregating or gathering had such political implications or legal ramifications. Without knowing that his marks implied gatherings, I imagined star clusters and I like that they can be many things. When his color is bold it is more resonant. For me, sometimes, Lewis's works can be so controlled and almost claustrophobic at first, but then they slowly open up to reveal a celestial music.

JM: The dry transparency of the golden plum mist in Lewis's painting is so distinct from the flat opacity of the mint in your *Splendid* (plate 20). But you also create a sense of swarm through layered floating marks, and flecks of color. What guides the energy and atmosphere of *Splendid*?

SS: I see some correlation between us, but I feel more akin to other artists. For example, I feel an affinity to Joan Mitchell because of the free emotion and relationship to calligraphy in her brushwork and the visible journey of inner thought. Likewise to Alma Thomas for the lightness of being that some of her paintings also seem to strive toward. The gesture in my work is text, writing.

In *Splendid,* I was not thinking of congregations or gatherings of people. There was a romantic impulse developing, a form like a flowering bush or a thicket.

JM: I like your articulation of fluidity and live growth in *Splendid*. For me, its liveliness hovers, ungrounded. It could suggest an airy floating gathering, like starlings swirling in bouncing trajectories, or buoys bouncing on waves. This idea of floating is also manifest in the way the image action is texture—string, fabric, liquid lines—just above or upon the surface, instead of an image embedded within an illusionary picture plane. It hums.

I have a final question about power: How do you think people, societies, express "awe-inspiring or ungraspable" power?

SS: Through Art, through Love & Charity, the highest forms of human expression.

JM: You have been thinking a great deal about the potential power of the whimsical and joy. Where has this curiosity taken you?

SS: Curiosity implies it is outside myself and I am observing. I feel that I am allowing myself to experience and explore whimsy and joy, so that I could perhaps convey this to others and so that I can use it for my own evolution or enlightenment. At this point in my life, I feel that I want to use my "gifts" or whatever I have, my energy, toward bringing light to others.

JM: Well said. Talk about the experience.

SS: To allow oneself to experience Joy is to allow all the trials, heartbreaks and fragility of being human to meld with the beauty of being alive and being connected. It is not solely happiness. The combination of love, gratitude and compassion = joyful. People assume Joy is not serious, but frivolous and lighthearted in a way that is trite. In fact, Joy is to be filled, to feel whole and completed. It is not an easy state to come to, nor easy to maintain. Especially, for those who come from hardships of the inner city, who experience prejudice and subjugation.

As a Black artist, I am expected to not know Joy, or Fancy, or Whimsy, or be playful. These aspects of human life are not assigned to my identity and are not depicted. We are not supposed to frolic. And if we do, we risk being viewed as though we lack seri-ousness and may be ignoring injustices around us, but that is not the case with me.

JM: So Joy is a crucible, a wholeness, a resistance, and power?

SS: Yes, I like the word "crucible," because it is alchemy. I allow my works to go through stages of Agony, Pathos, and Epiphany. This for me engages the whole and in the resolution of a work, I strive to find Joy in the experience of life or transmute my experiences. My works don't always reach it. There is still a melancholy and nostalgia that permeates them but they are reaching for it. I think it is important to claim and I do believe it is empowering for us all.

For me, Black Lives and All Lives Matter. For me, "Everything Counts in Large Amounts" and I extract it, channel it. My life in Baltimore, my travels of the world, my experiences with indigenous elders, family and friends, the daily remarks and actions that belittle my existence as a Black woman, and the daily moments of kindness, beauty and heroism: I evoke it all. I render it to canvas and glue fragments of it together. I leave traces of my soul and words that affirm my existence. I have to.

This conversation is an edited compilation of correspondence between Jen Mergel and Shinique Smith during June and July 2015.

Note

1. A. C. Bhaktivedanta Swami Prabhupada, *KRSNA: The Supreme Personality of Godhead* (Los Angeles: ISKCON, 1970).

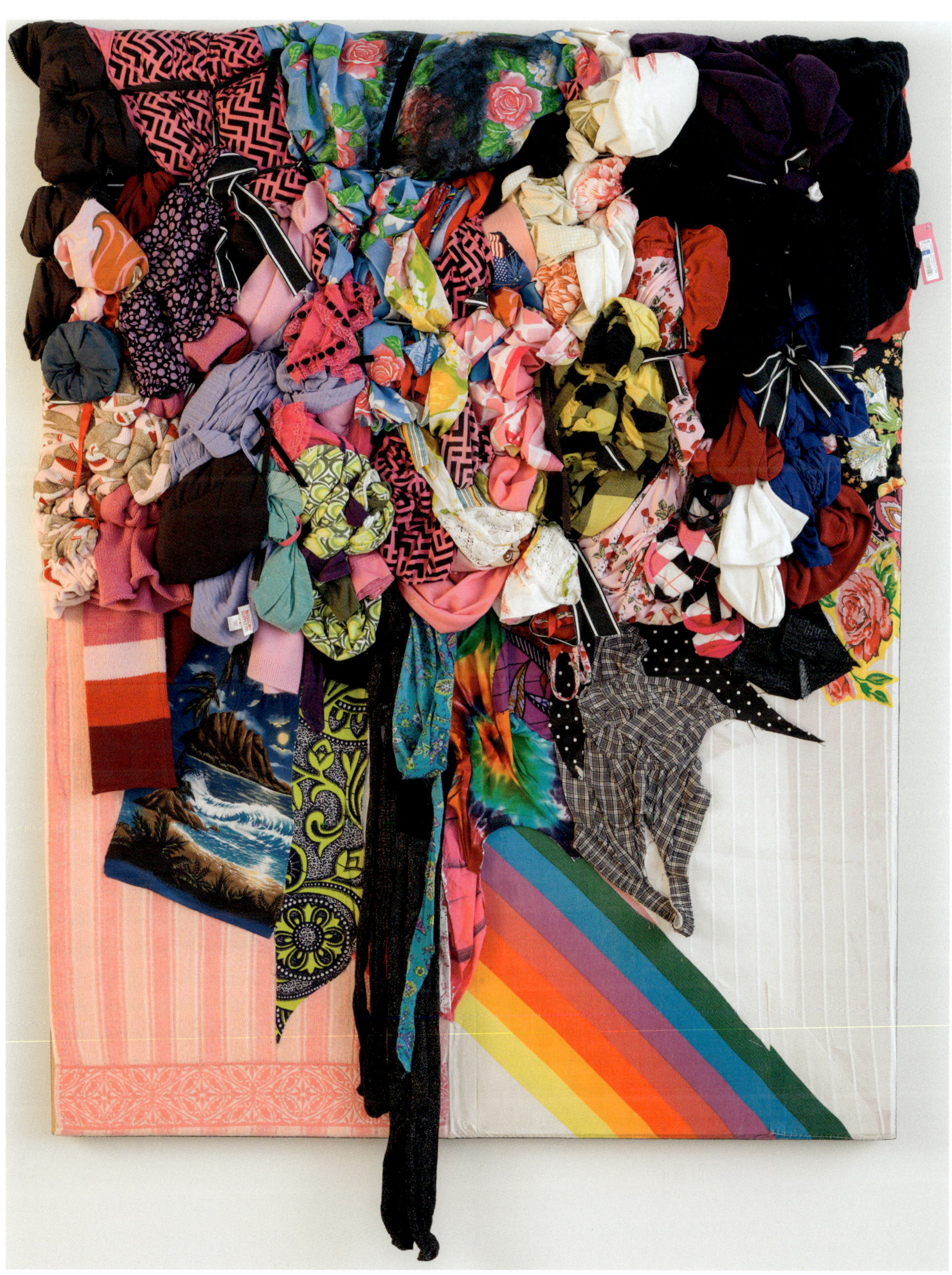

16   *Bright Matter*
2013

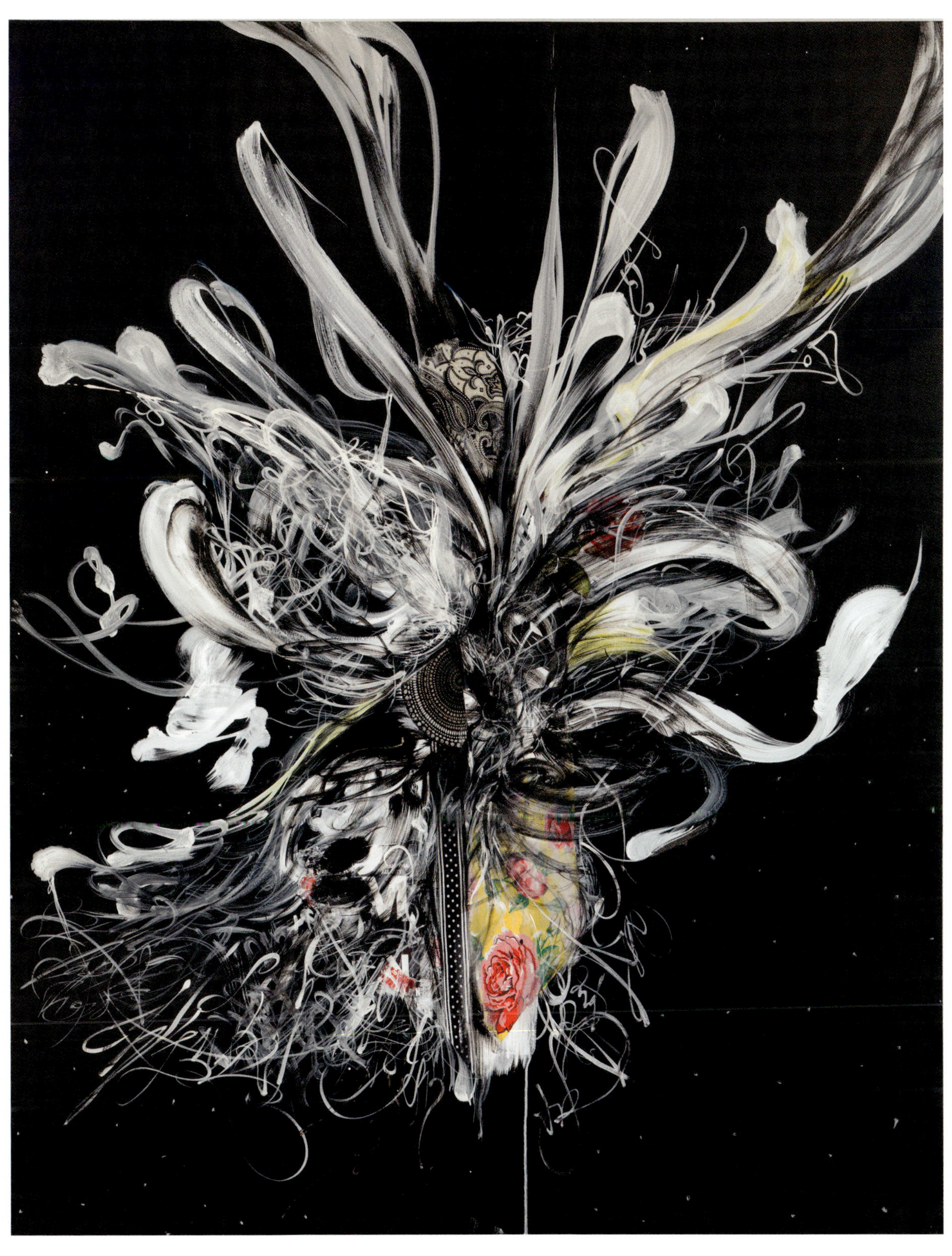

17   *Right through You*
2014

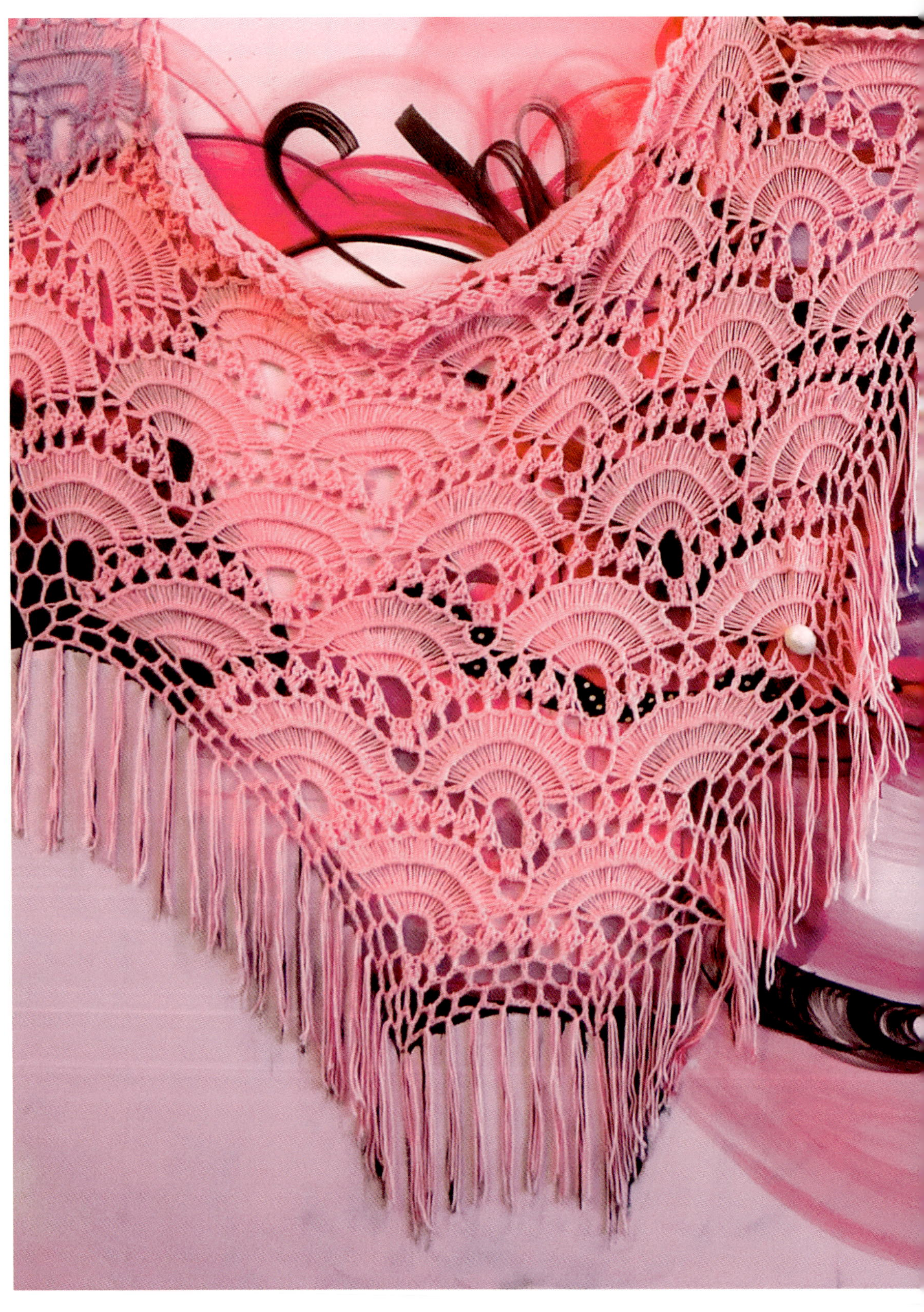

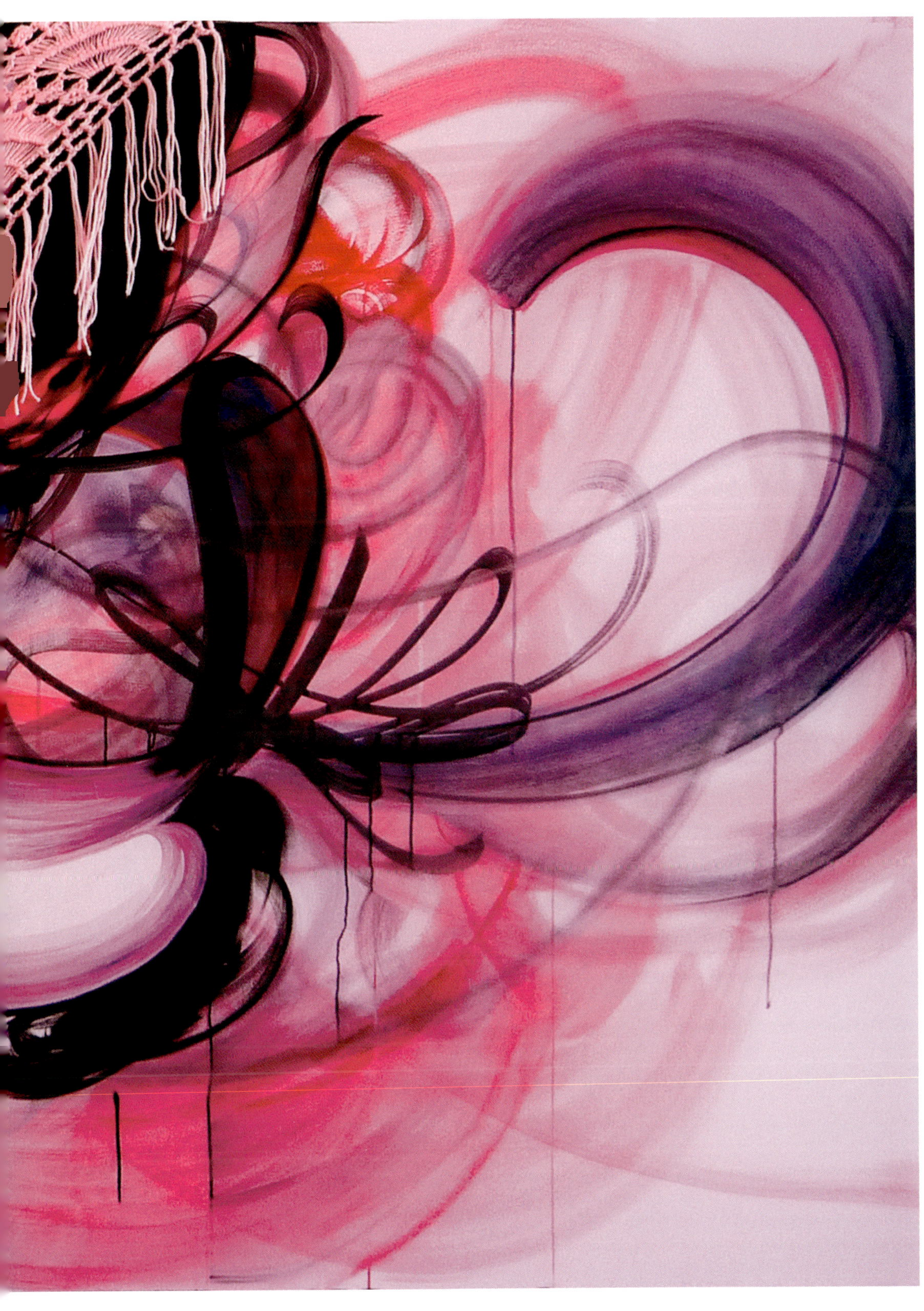

18   *Of a Particular Perfume*
2011

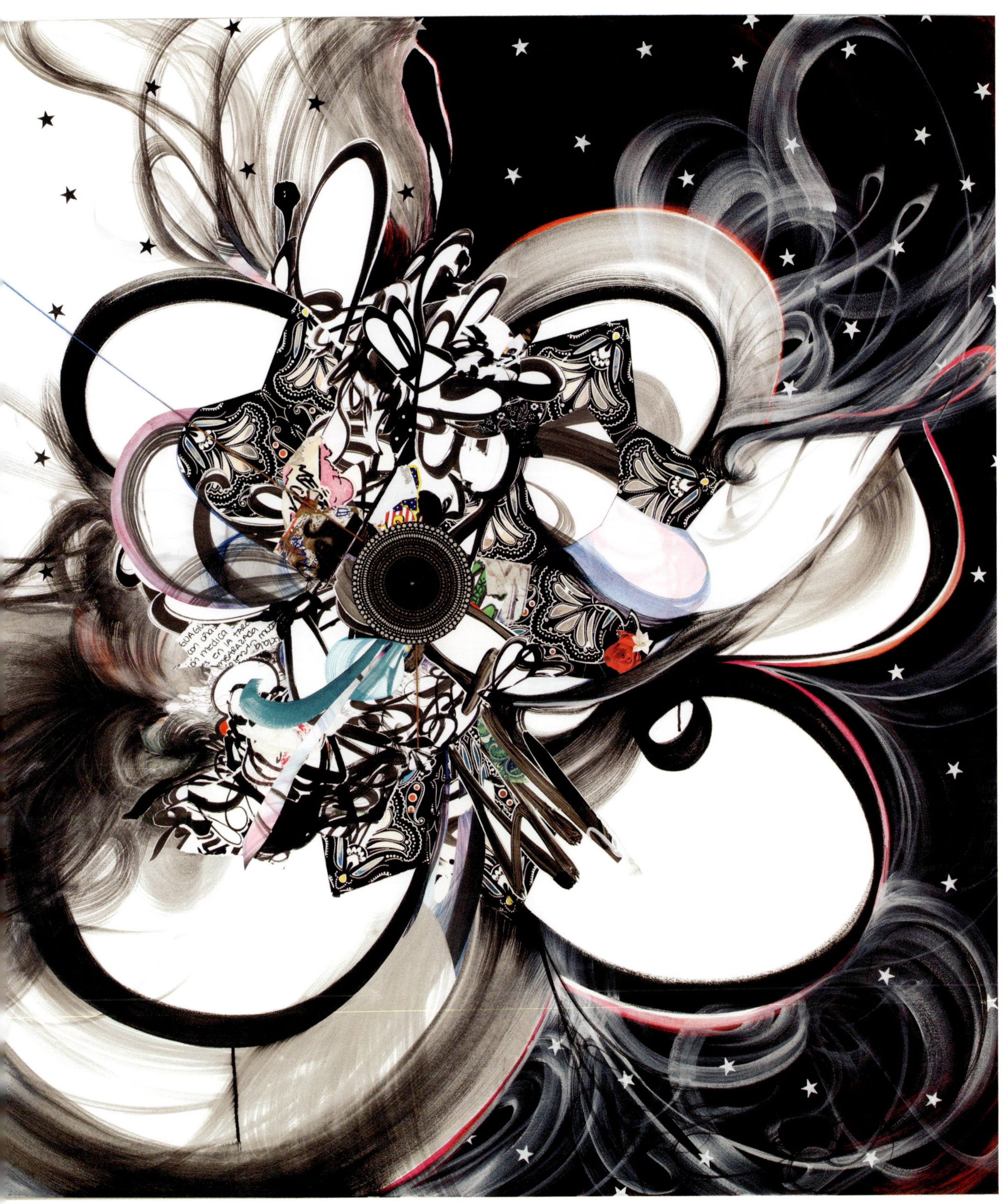

19 *No Key, No Question*
2013

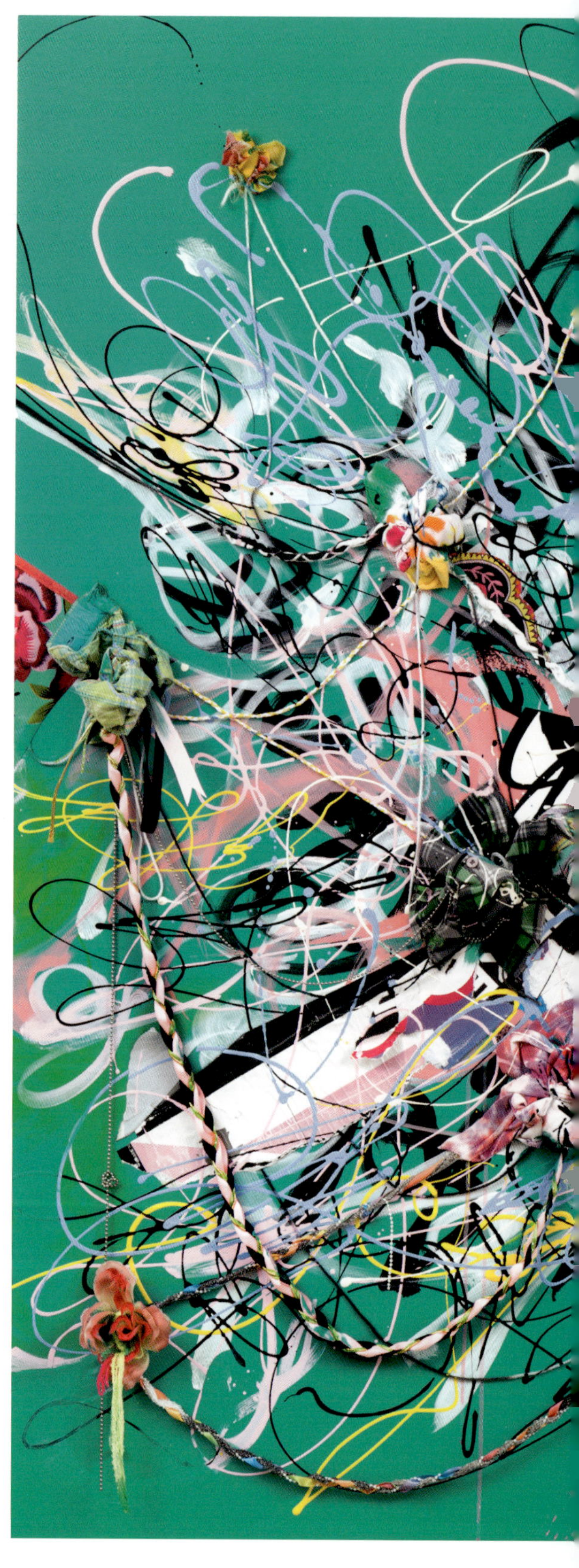

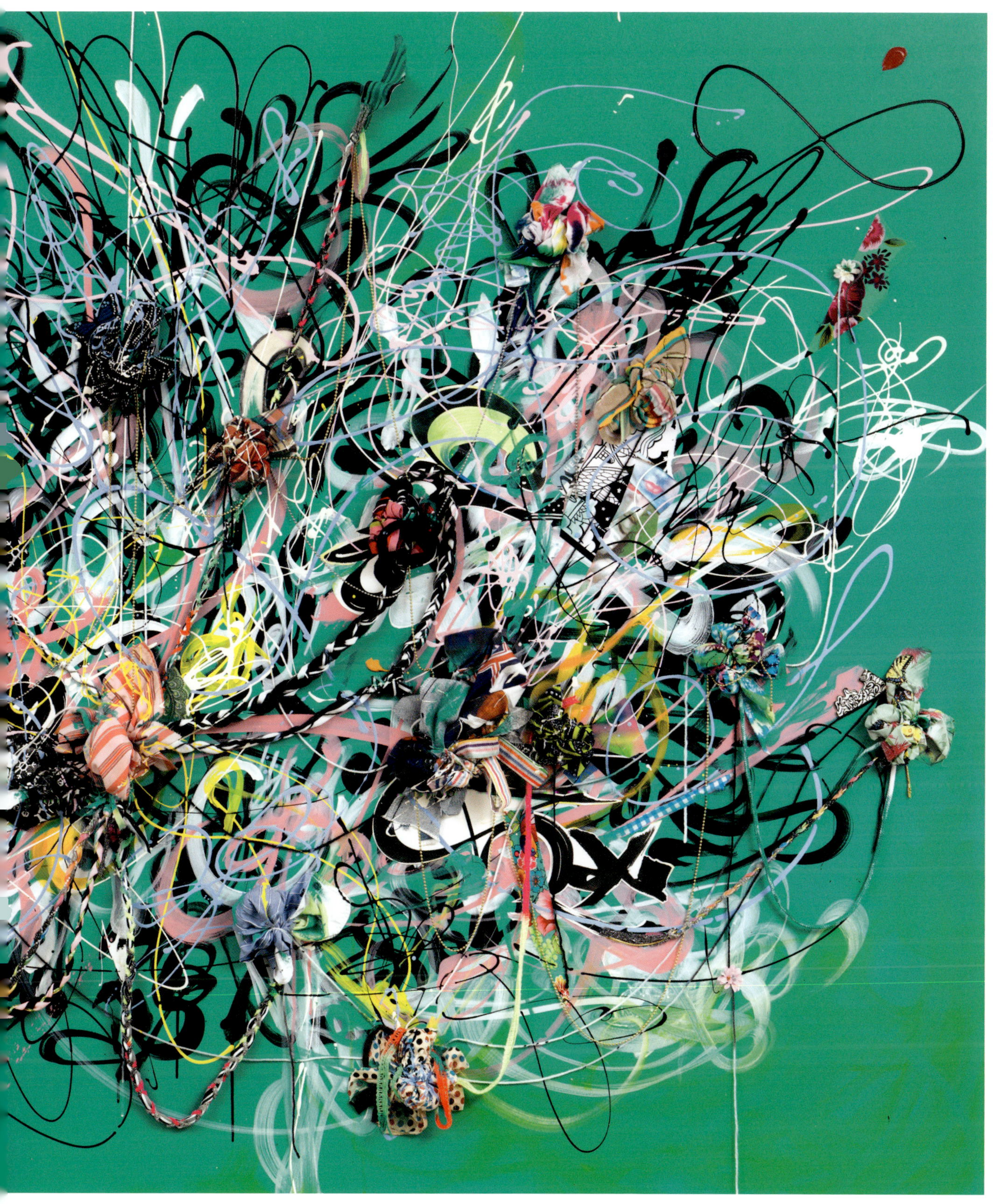

20 *Splendid*
2014

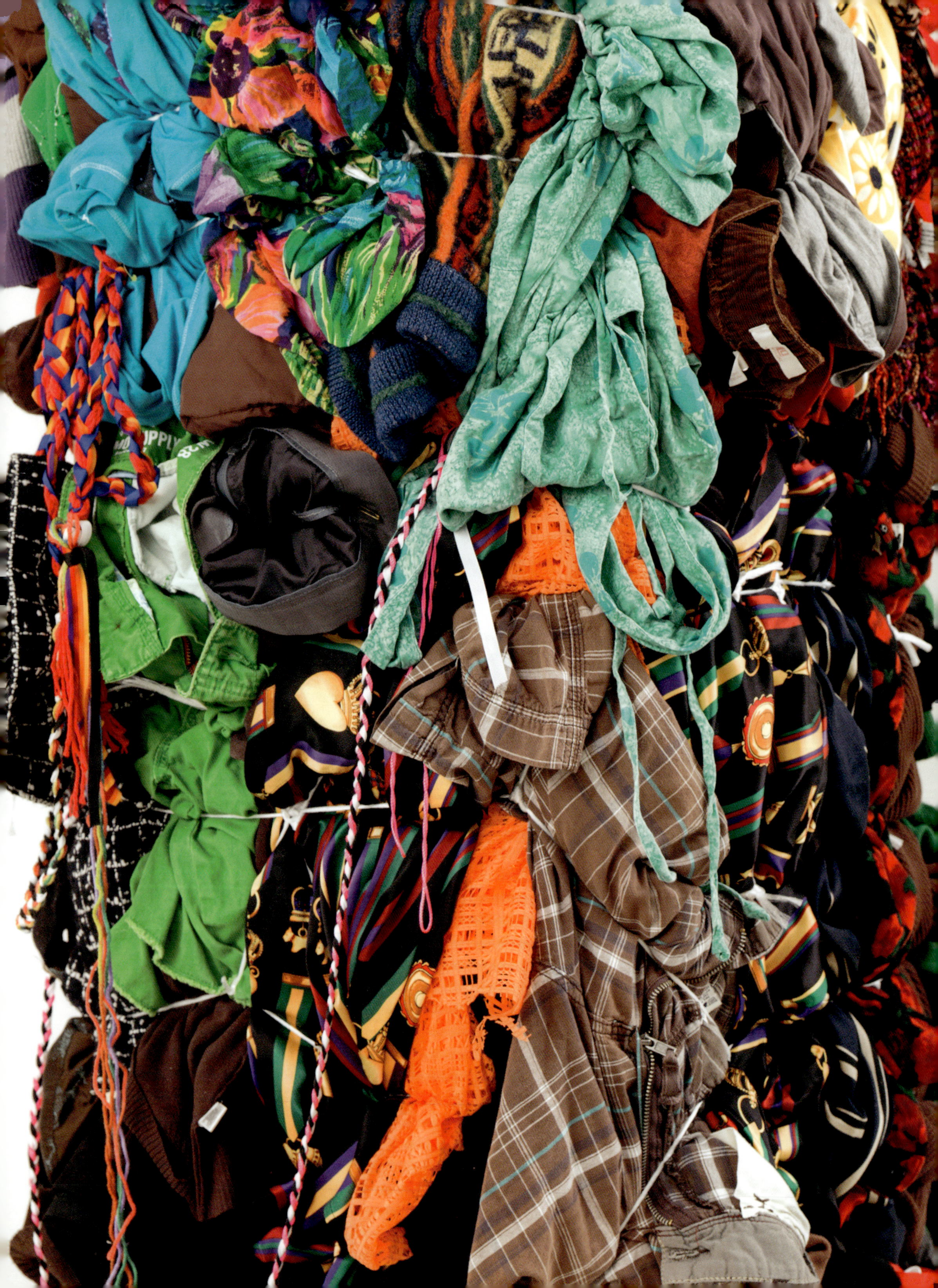

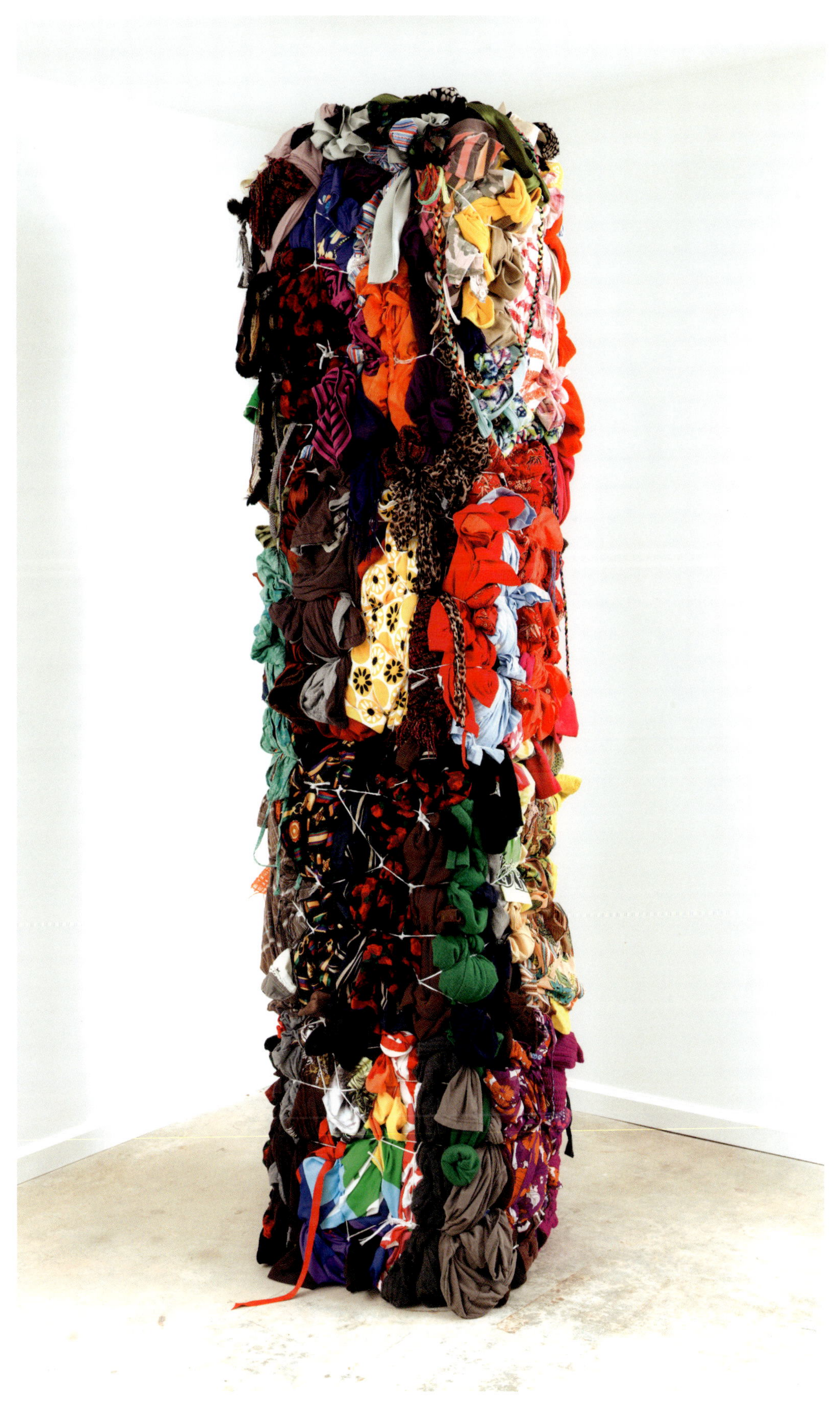

21   *Bale Variant No. 0023 (Totem)*
2014

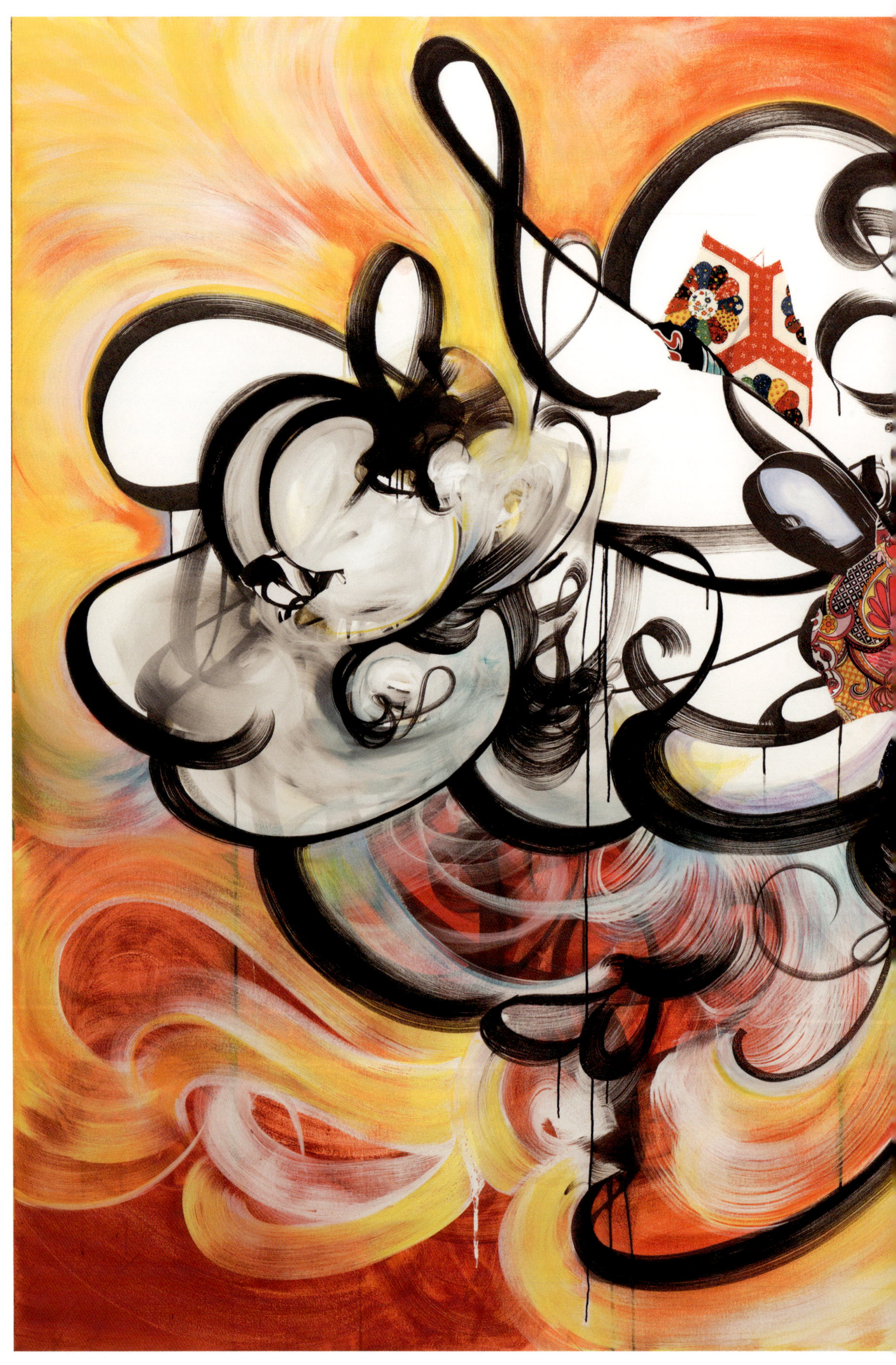

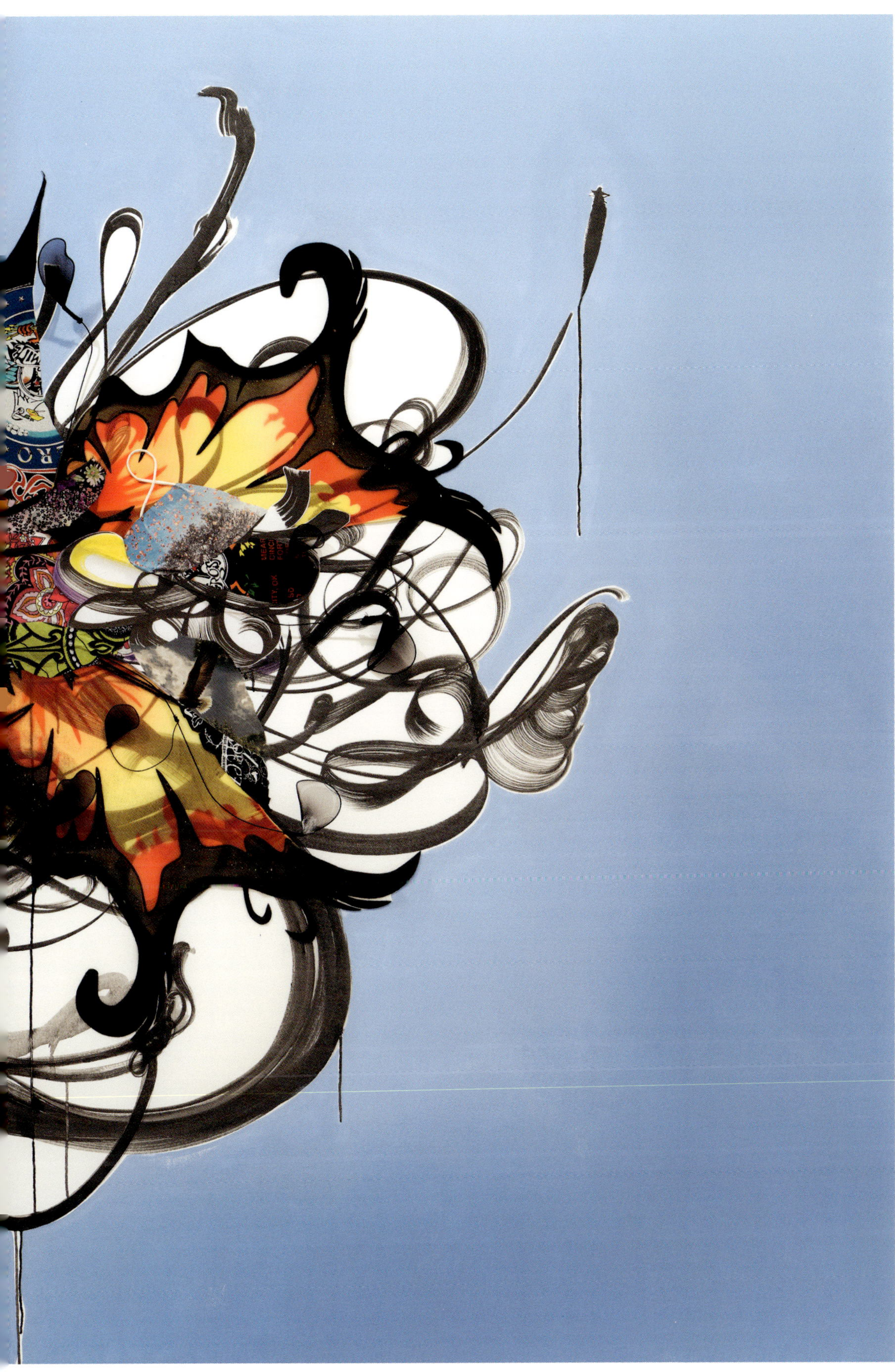

22   *The Power to See*
      2012

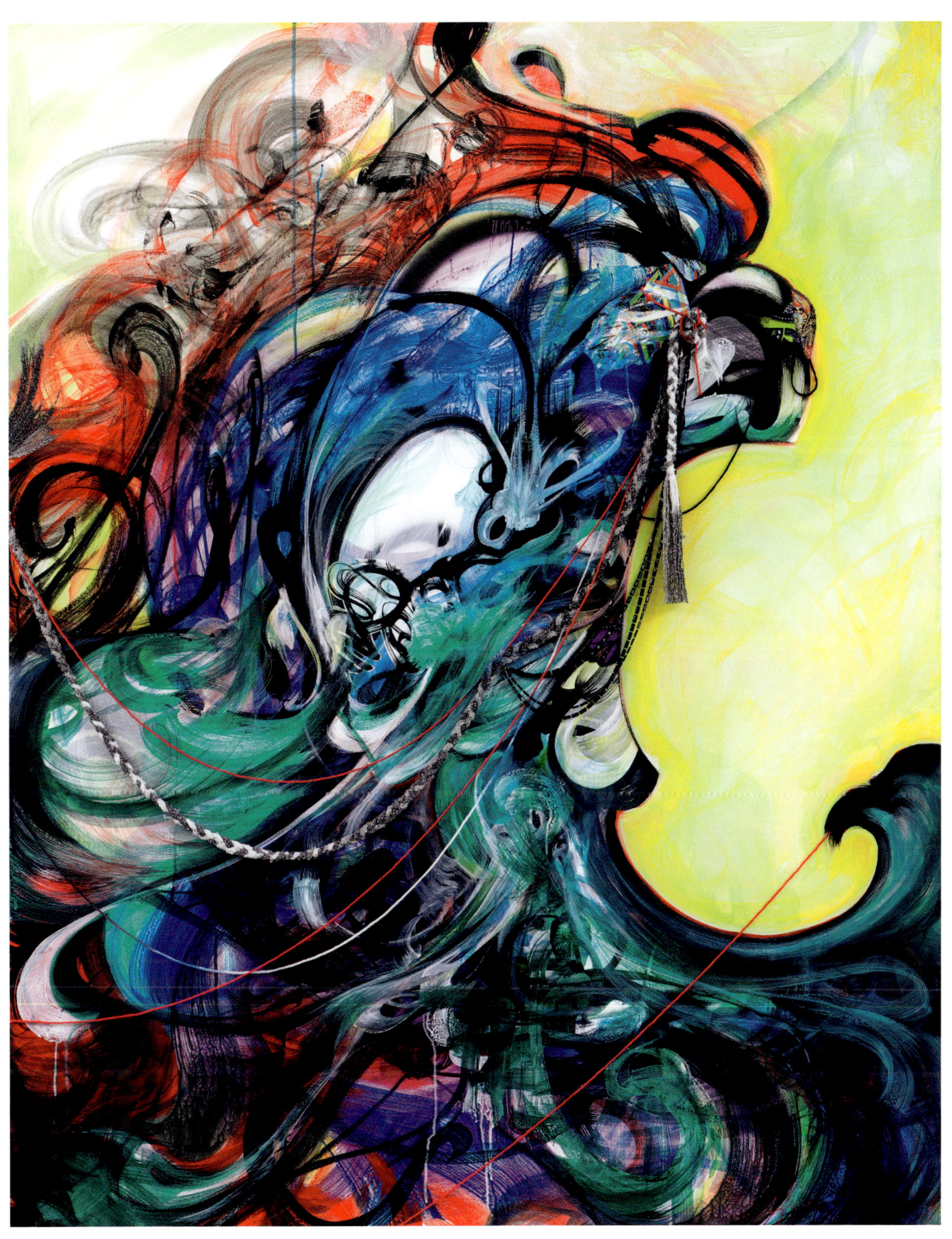

23   *With wings, newly made of water*
2014

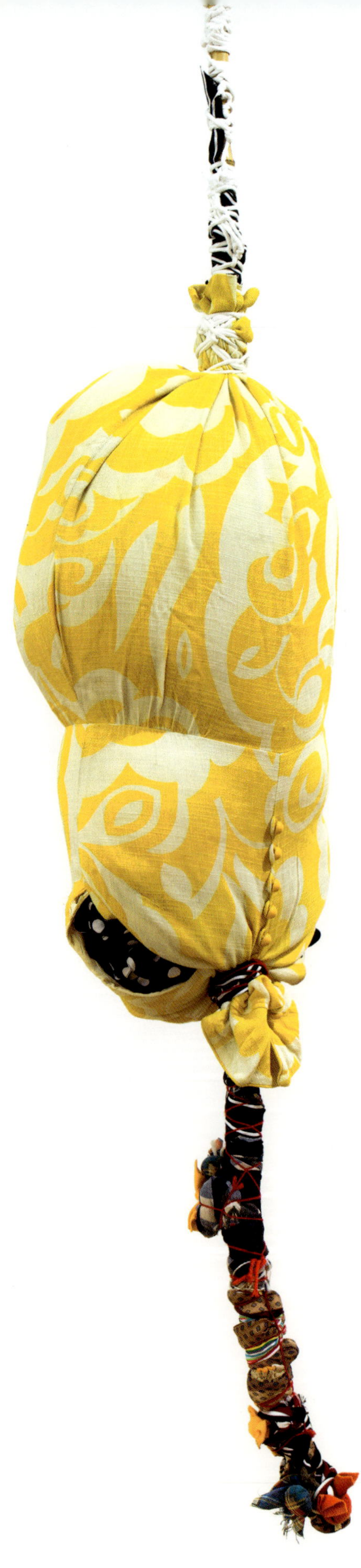

24   *This Yellow Shell*
2013

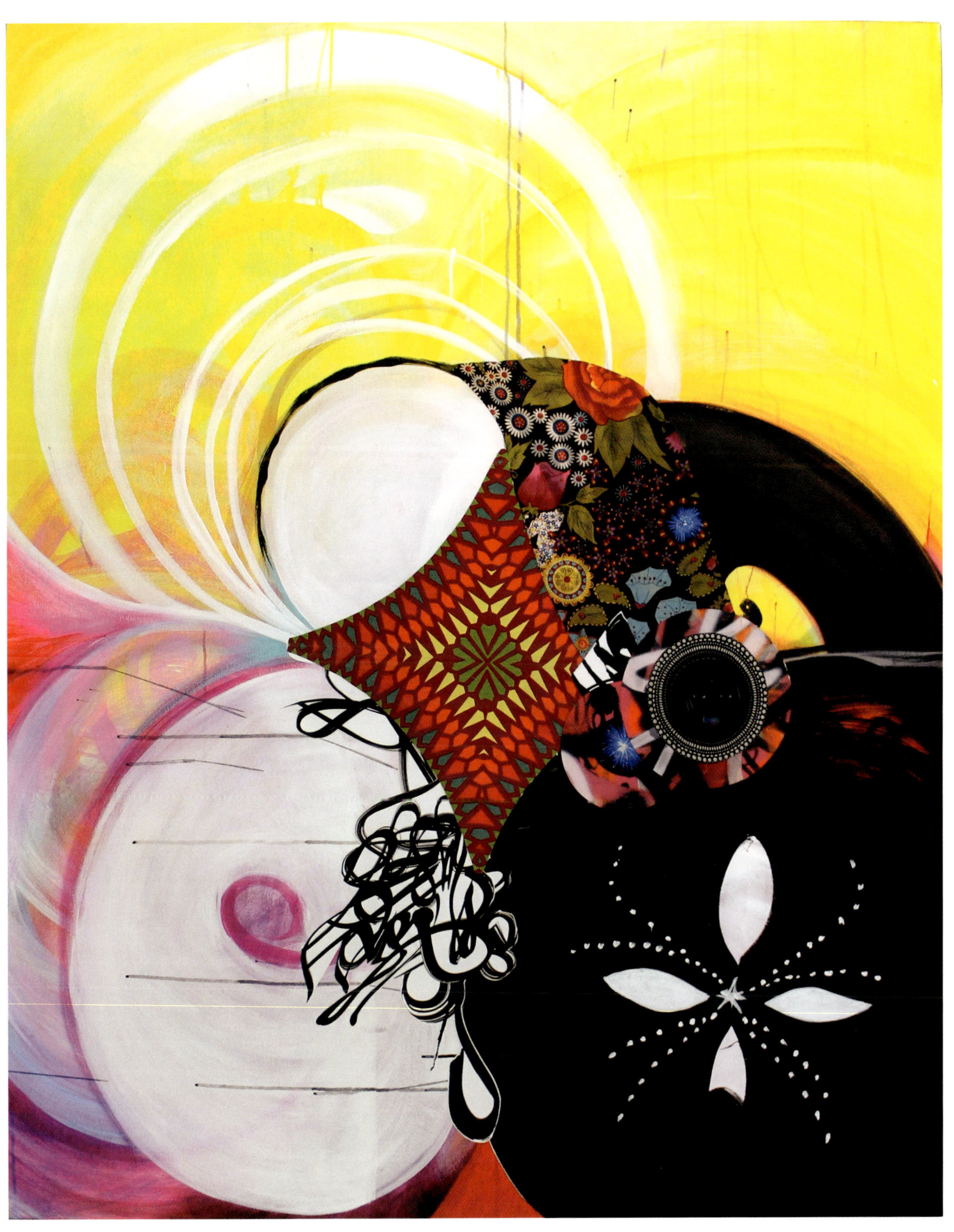

25 *Seven Moons*
2013

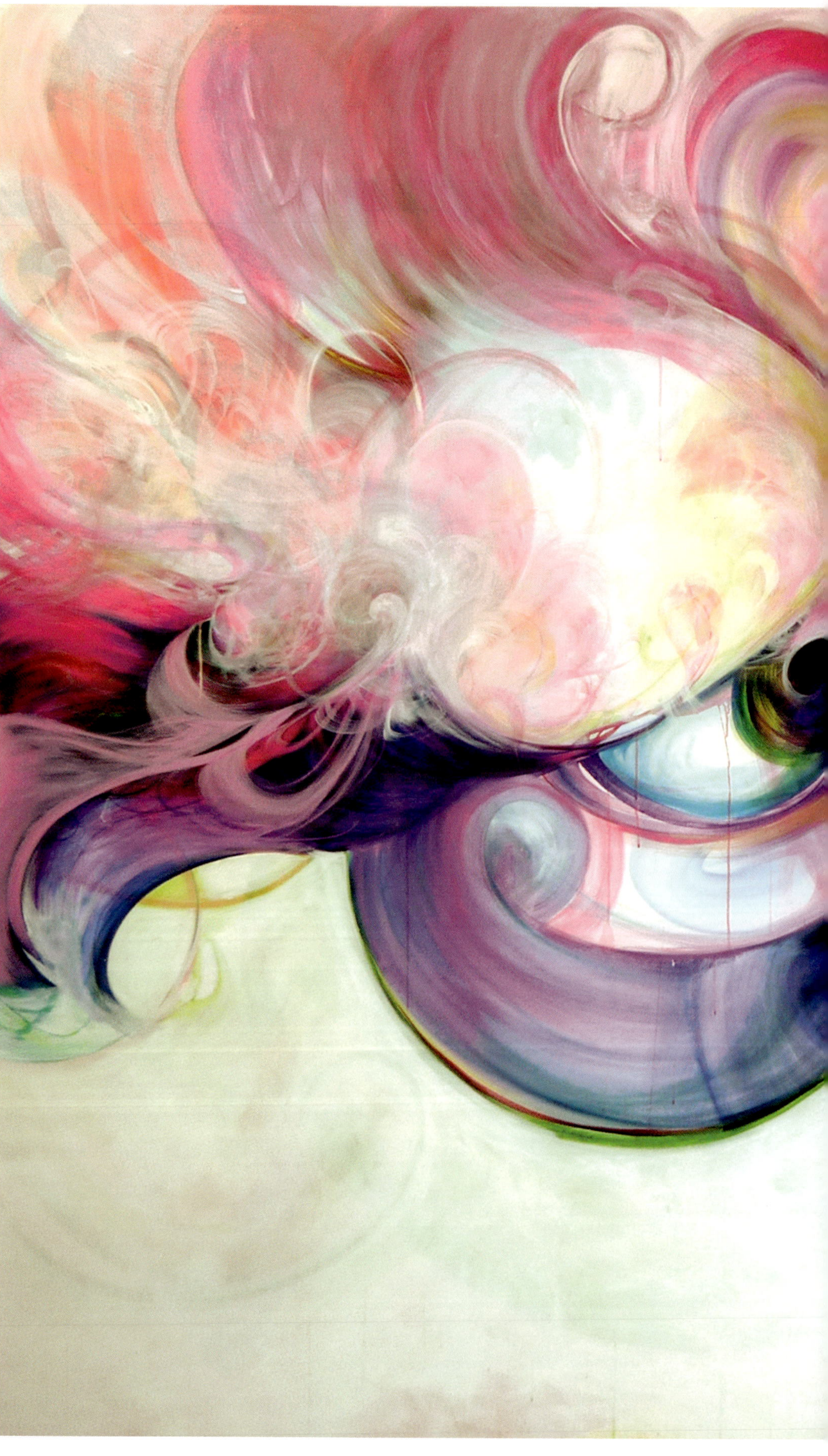

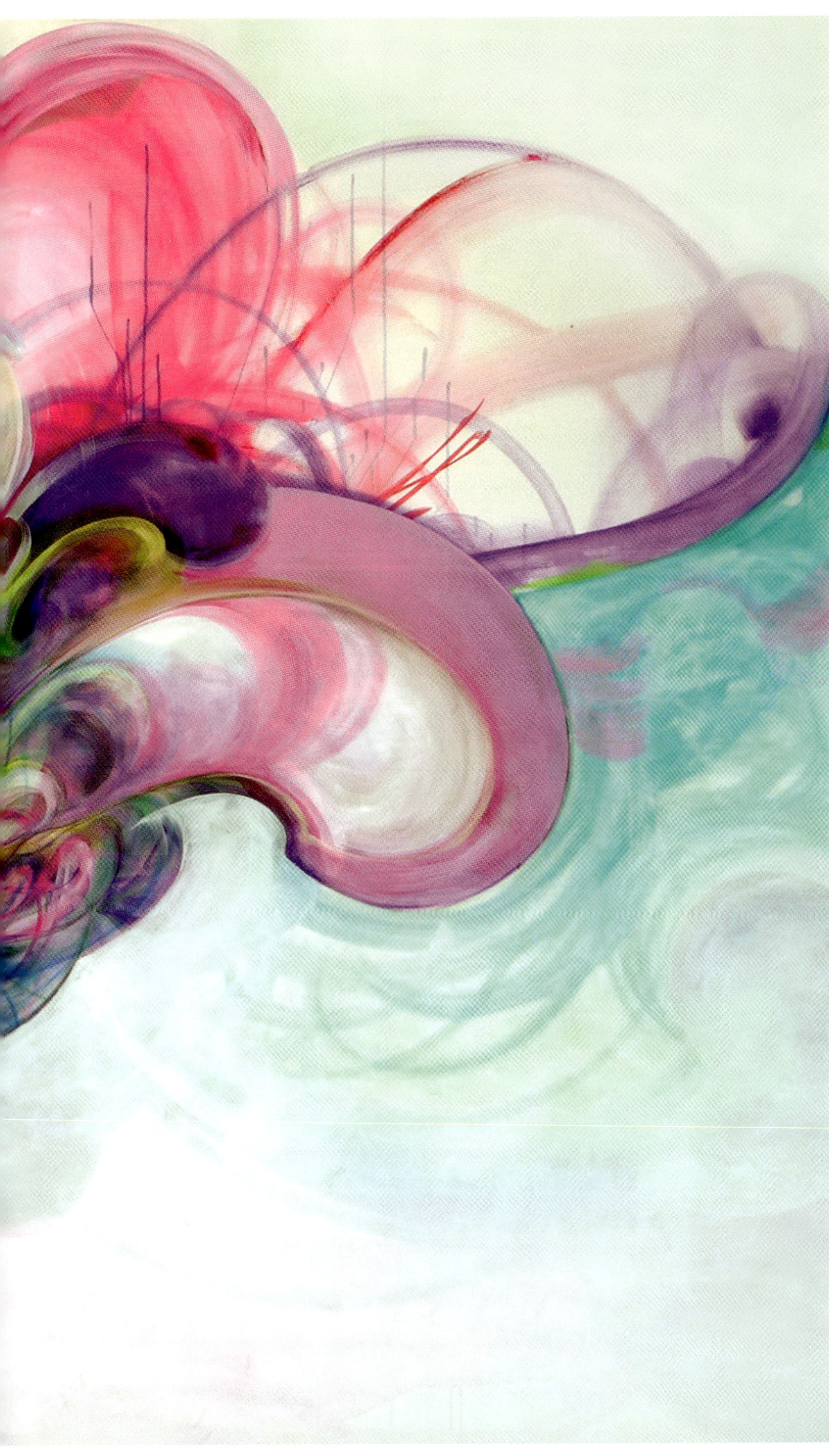

26   *Majesty*
2012

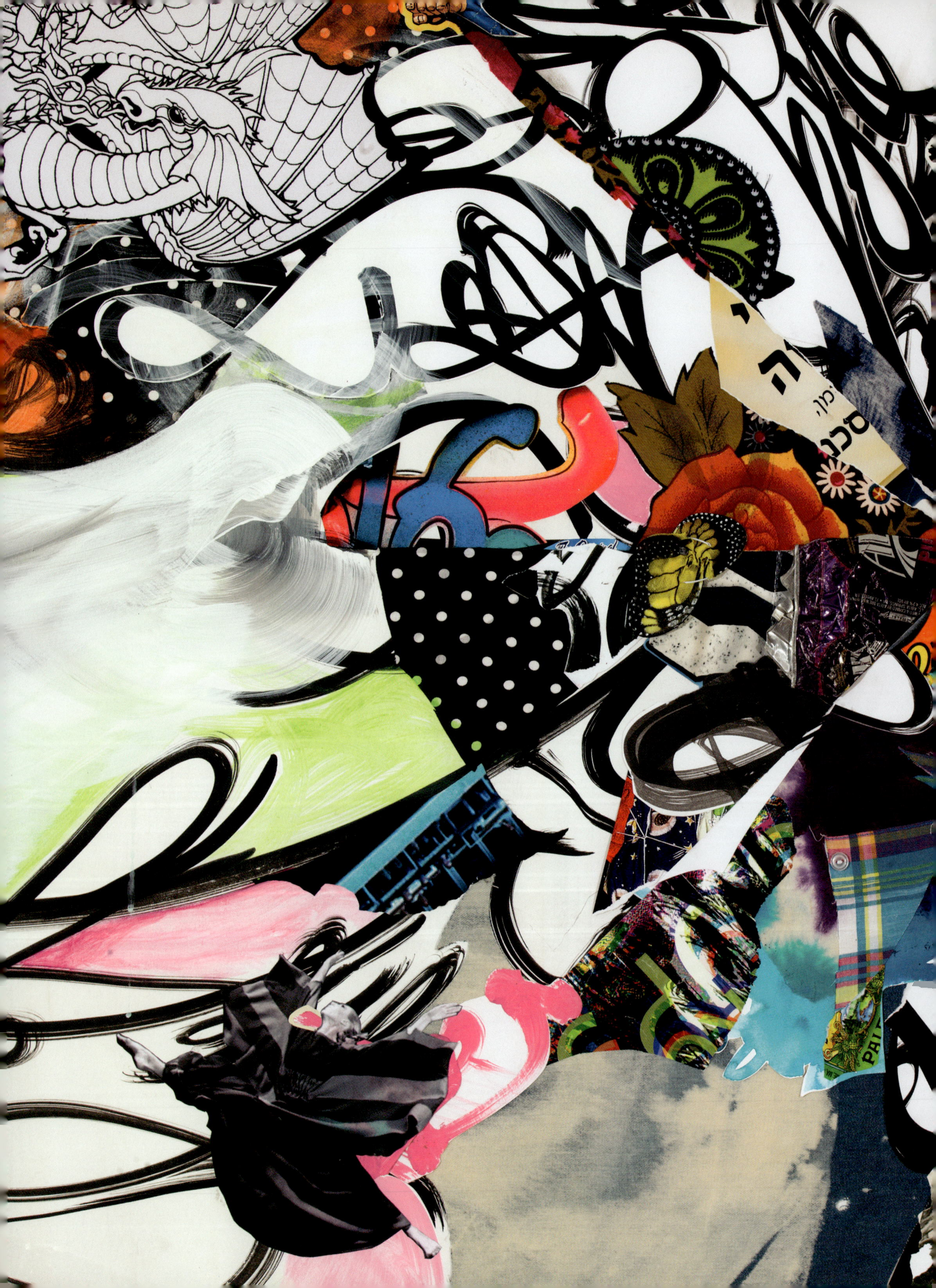

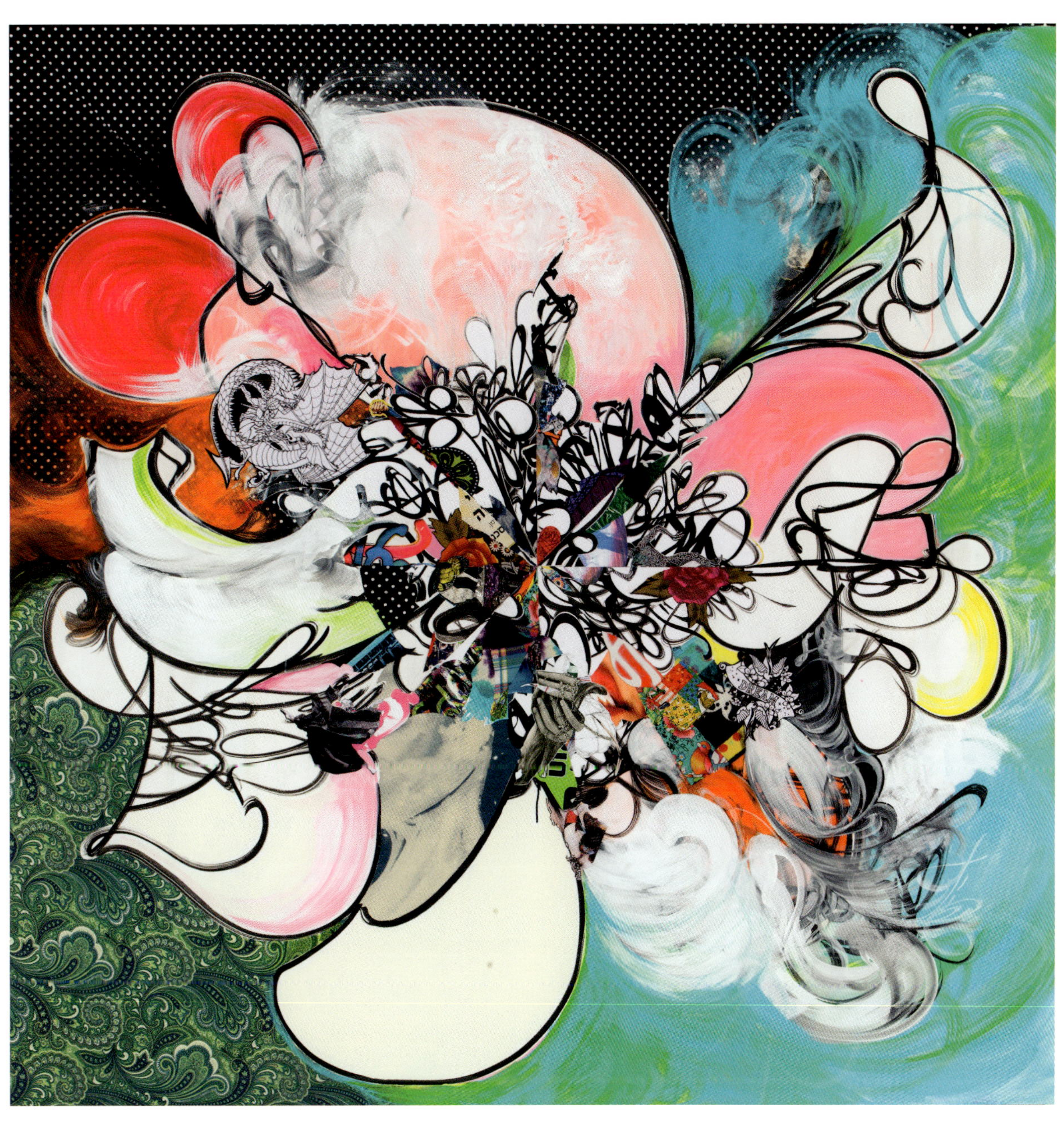

27 **Gravity of Love**
2013

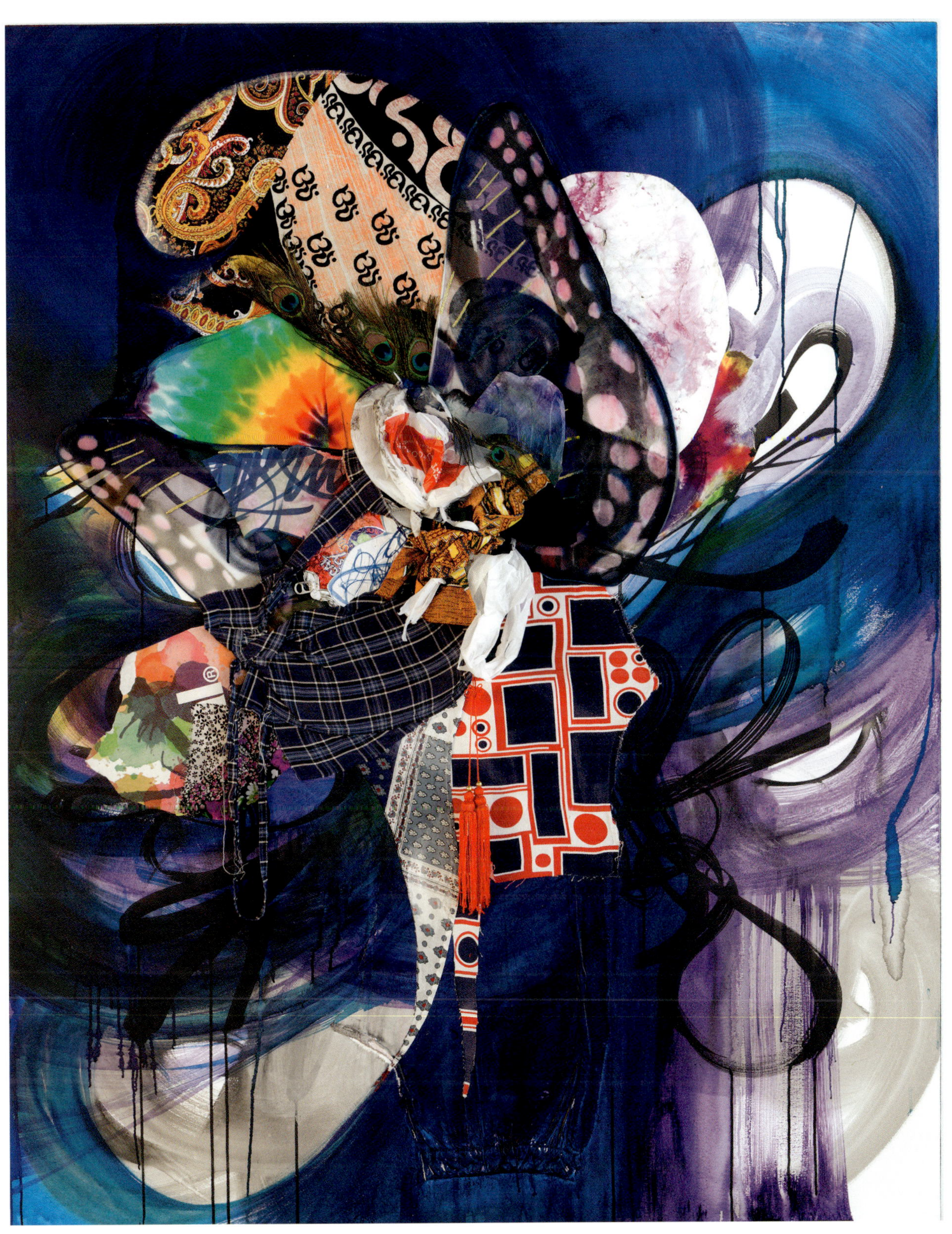

28   *Through native streets*
2011

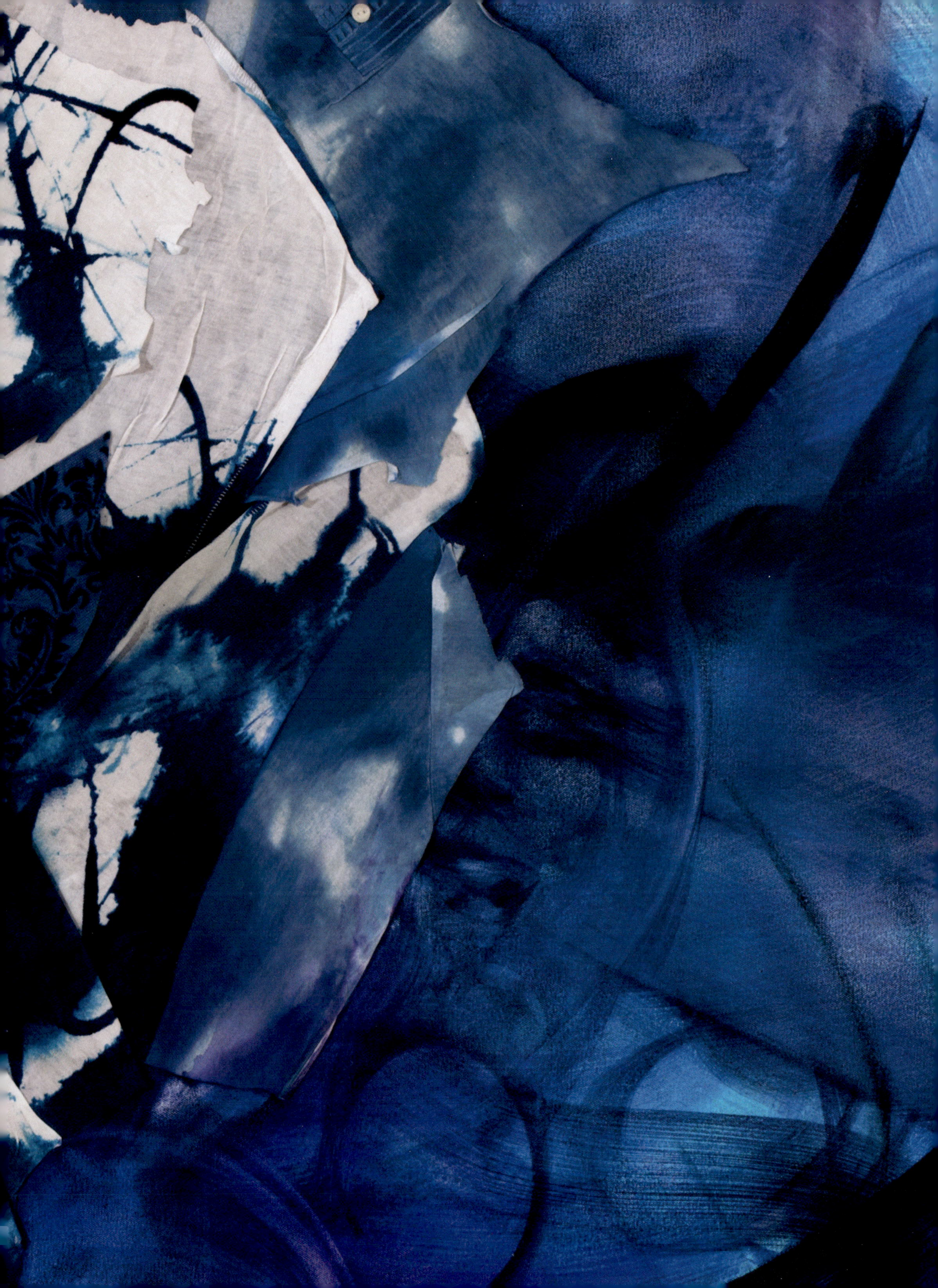

Black Wonder and Rainbows

Shinique Smith

I am the woman who holds up the sky.
My feet are planted in all generations.
My roots go deep into melted rock.
I walk through darkest night
Wearing starlight in my hair.
I am the woman who holds up the sky.
The rainbow runs through my eyes.
The sun makes a path to my womb.
My thoughts are in the shape of clouds
But my words are yet to come.[1]

Titles. Titles such as these stir my curiosity and imagination: *The Black Unicorn* poems (Audre Lorde), *Bold as Love* (Jimi Hendrix), *Cotton Candy on a Rainy Day* (Nikki Giovanni), *The Giving Tree* (Shel Silverstein), "Howling Self" (The Duke Spirit), *Song of Myself* (Walt Whitman), *Wild Seed* (Octavia Butler), *A Wrinkle in Time* (Madeleine L'Engle), "She Walks in Beauty" (Lord Byron), *Walking through Mirrors* (Brian Keith Jackson), *Their Eyes Were Watching God* (Zora Neale Hurston), *Up to and Including Her Limits* (Carolee Schneemann), *Stars in My Pocket Like Grains of Sand* (Samuel R. Delany).

And then I read further and these titles give me more. Words inspire me to contemplate my relationship to them. I bask in them and cull associations from different points in my life that they evoke; other things I've read, songs I've heard, places I've been, and the feelings that arise.

Poetic language has always seemed like a higher form of communication to me with its ability to lyrically capture a moment, a story, a life in a few words. Metaphorical language allows one's mind room to visualize and feel. I strive for the same conveyance of wonder in my work.

The language of collage is like structuring a poem, piecing together words and phrases into complete rhythmic verse. Working a composition and finding visual and conceptual connections between the materials while maintaining an economic balance between each element is a complex equation. I take the words and use them like waves of energy to transcribe emotion and bind together scraps and cuttings of fabric and paper, fodder and bric-a-brac, in order to make a new whole.

*W*hen I was a child, my mother and I lived with my grandparents in a typical Baltimore row house. We were a close family and the things I read, saw, and experienced then contribute greatly to the way I view the world now.

Each house in the neighborhood was connected to neighbors' yards and porches with either a street or an alleyway between each row of homes. Many things transpired when I played alone in the backyard. It was a small patch of green enclosed by chain-link fencing with a concrete sidewalk running along the border. I used to sit on my rock. My family called it "Shinique's rock." I believed it was a boulder when I was small, but when I returned as an adult I found it was a blob of cement. I sat there for hours looking out on my grandfather's vegetable garden, miraculously filled with corn stalks and pumpkins and other delicacies in the middle of the city, and dream. I would imagine myself in other realms.

The idea of a mini-universe has always inspired me and sometimes I would imagine myself to be as *wee* as a "Smurf," and I experienced the yard from that tiny perspective. There was a hole in the sidewalk about the size of a piece of copy paper that filled with water when it rained. I would squat at the edge and observe a miniature lake

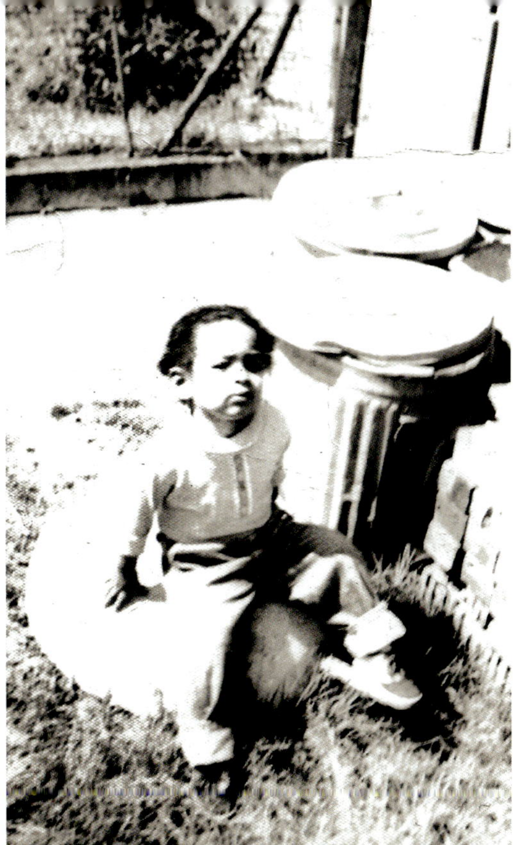

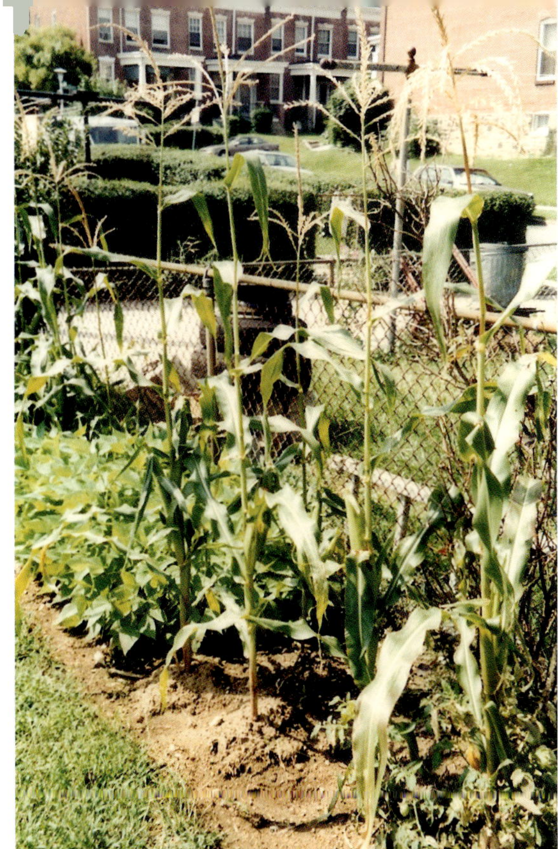

filled with plant life, bits of copper, dirt, and stone. I wondered who might live there and in my heart it felt like a landscape that I could travel within. When I showed my mother what I had found and explained it to her, she marveled along with me and said it was a "microcosm."

This was a mystical word to me, which spoke of small unseen and unexplored realms. From this, I developed an affinity for miniature landscapes and scenes. In my work, I consider the effects that scale, weight, and gravity may have on the viewer. Each of my sculptures is a microcosm of grander memories and circumstances, containing 10 to 100 or more individual parts.

The clothing and objects that I use in my work are collected over time. They come from my home, from my friends and family, and from places I've travelled. Some bits and pieces I have had for 10 years or more. Some pieces of clothing are irreplace-able, so I have savored them over time—using a little here and a little there until just one sleeve or collar is left. The history of each object is inherited and absorbed into whole clusters of color and relative meaning.

My bundled sculptures are like conglomerate rocks that become cemented together with bits of rock, sand, and shell over time to create a new separate form. These thoughts intrigue me, as do the ideals we place on garments and things we acquire.

We consume, desire, live, love, and let go of things that become outworn or ill-fitting, or when the memories associated with them become distasteful. Or, our things simply go adrift into the American void of plastic bags floating down streets like urban tumbleweeds. There is something grotesque, gluttonous, pitiable, and beautifully fragile about the way we associate and present ourselves through our clothing and objects. Is it human nature?

When we're young, we're taught to admire and share our objects through show-n-tell. We learn what basic needs are, like food, shelter, and clothing, whether these needs are fulfilled or not. Then we learn to acquire beyond need and according to status or desire. I think we're all connected by our relationship to "stuff" and things. Whether we embrace Consumerism or loathe these impulses and the effects they have on the world, things-n-stuff define us.

Recently, I was thinking about things I shared for show-n-tell as a child, things that I've held on to and still cherish. I recall vividly interacting with them and the feeling of wonder they encouraged. I especially marveled at my Sesame Street playhouse, which looked just like the set, except it had stickers that were stand-ins for real life. If I could encapsulate when my aesthetic sensibilities evolved, I would say it was during my childhood—as I played with my Sesame Street playhouse in my grandmother's living room, which she had decorated with an array of tiny teacups and

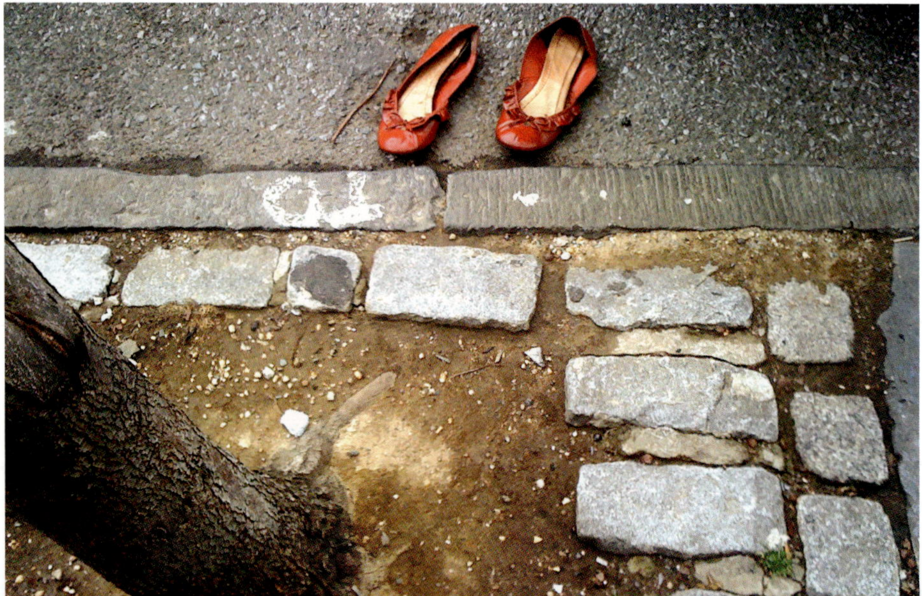

Fig. 3

Shinique Smith. *Red shoes in Brooklyn*, 2009. Digital print. One of many images taken by the artist of objects encountered in her daily life, which are used for inspiration and become artworks themselves.

glass keepsakes I wasn't allowed to touch, among floral pillows and brocade sofa that harmonized somehow under Romare Bearden posters depicting Black life through collage. As my family sat around me, watching the junk dealers of *Sanford and Son* on TV, I think I began to see life as a collage of figures, patterns, objects, and experiences.

My mother's own creativity fostered my awareness of clothing and fabric through her fashion designs. When I was growing up, she created amazing sculptural garments that mixed textures like crochet with denim. She studied fashion design in Paris, where the artist and designer Erté became one of her mentors. His whimsical graphics directly influenced my hand, as he was the first artist whose work I tried to copy as a child.

In high school, I was struck by Robert Rauschenberg's work *Canyon* at the Baltimore Museum of Art (now at MoMA) and how it came to life in such a physical way with paint and a majestic yet abject bald eagle. His combine *Bed* at MoMA first showed me that a quilt could exist as color and retain its identity as an everyday object (see page 3). Later, in grad school, seeing *The Quilts of Gee's Bend* at the Whitney was also affecting. Several quilts were made from the work pants of the quilters' husbands. It was endearing to experience the reuse of common items like my granddad's pants. I was floored by one quilt that still held the impressions of two bodies, of the couple that slept under the quilt for years before it was hung in the museum.

All these moments, along with the influence of school, travel, and the experiences of my life and surroundings, continued my fascination with clothing and objects—these things we have in common and imbue with meaning. I started using these materials flatly. Then ruffling them and tying them up into bundles made sense to me as an act and as a form. When I first began making these objects, I had the impulse to apply the same gesture to my body, with clothes not worn but bound onto myself until I was inside the sculpture.

The materials I collect reflect my relationships—my desires and attractions. Fabrics and objects that allude to pastoral landscapes are romantically linked to my dreams of utopia, for example, and I use paisleys and brocades that remind me of reading Scheherazade's vivid tales of princes, genies, and thieves illustrated in Antonio Lopez's *Tales from the Thousand and One Nights* as a child.

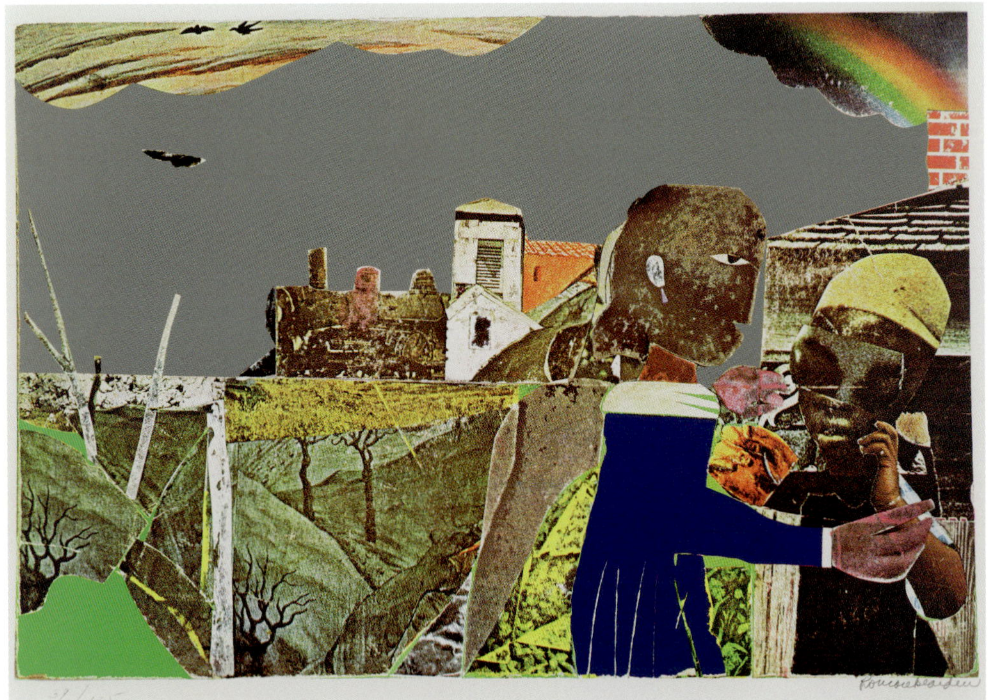

My work probably says more about me than I realize.

The works I make are improvisational and I use an organic approach in the studio with a phrase, color, or pattern as a starting point. Beginning a work without knowing what the outcome will be rekindles that feeling of discovery I had as a child.

I find connections between the materials in the midst of the work and, as they form, I learn how to tie them together and where to layer objects or paint. I like working with these materials for that reason. I'm inspired by connections we have through our relationship to things like socks. Basic needs, as simple as socks, can be taken for granted in Western society and one's relationship to them varies according to climate and economic circumstance—one pair may be all that one can afford or even none at all.

There are invisible connections that I perceive and tie together with color, shape, idea, and symbolism. Emotion is directly bound to the work with calligraphy, rope, and ribbon. These are lines between the viewer and me that weave together dreams and thoughts.

Someone once told me that my brushstrokes reminded them of kite strings. This remark resonated and set me on a tangent about Strings. Open strings—Heartstrings—Super strings—that bind people and their histories with my own, and I continue to dream invisible lines strung throughout the world connecting us all.

I like to discover things for myself even though I may interpret them incorrectly. I let my imagination wander freely and allow myself to imbue things with magical properties. One might call it perceiving the world with a sense of wonder. The words "Black Wonder" come to mind. I am not certain exactly what that means, but as an idea these words encourage me.

I was told once that "Black girls don't frolic" in reference to one of my video works with dancers. This statement sparked a resistance within me that drives me to draw beauty from cast-off belongings and the downcast aspects of life. I find joy in this way of seeing.

I also like to think about that time before tragedy and judgment existed, a time when the most meager chunk of cement next to a trashcan could be a place for magical thinking. I reach for harmony and balanced chaos, and for a hopeful conclusion, like when I was a child sitting on my rock in my grandparents' backyard.

Note

1. "I am the woman who holds up the sky." © 1979 Nancy C. Wood, reprinted from *War Cry on a Prayer Feather*, courtesy of the Nancy Wood Literary Trust, NancyWood.com.

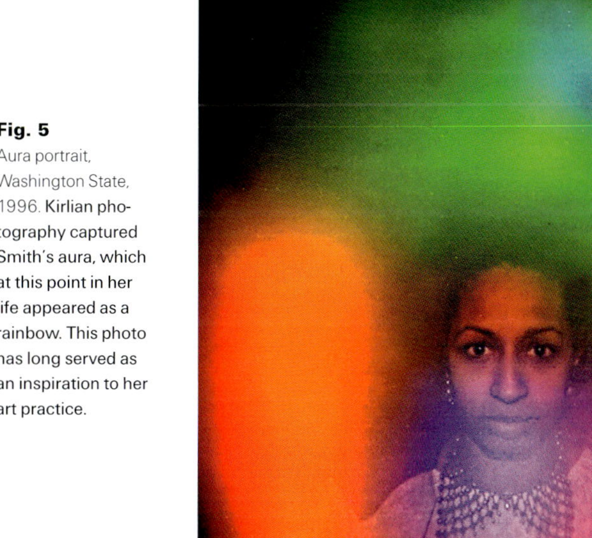

Fig. 5
Aura portrait, Washington State, 1996. Kirlian photography captured Smith's aura, which at this point in her life appeared as a rainbow. This photo has long served as an inspiration to her art practice.

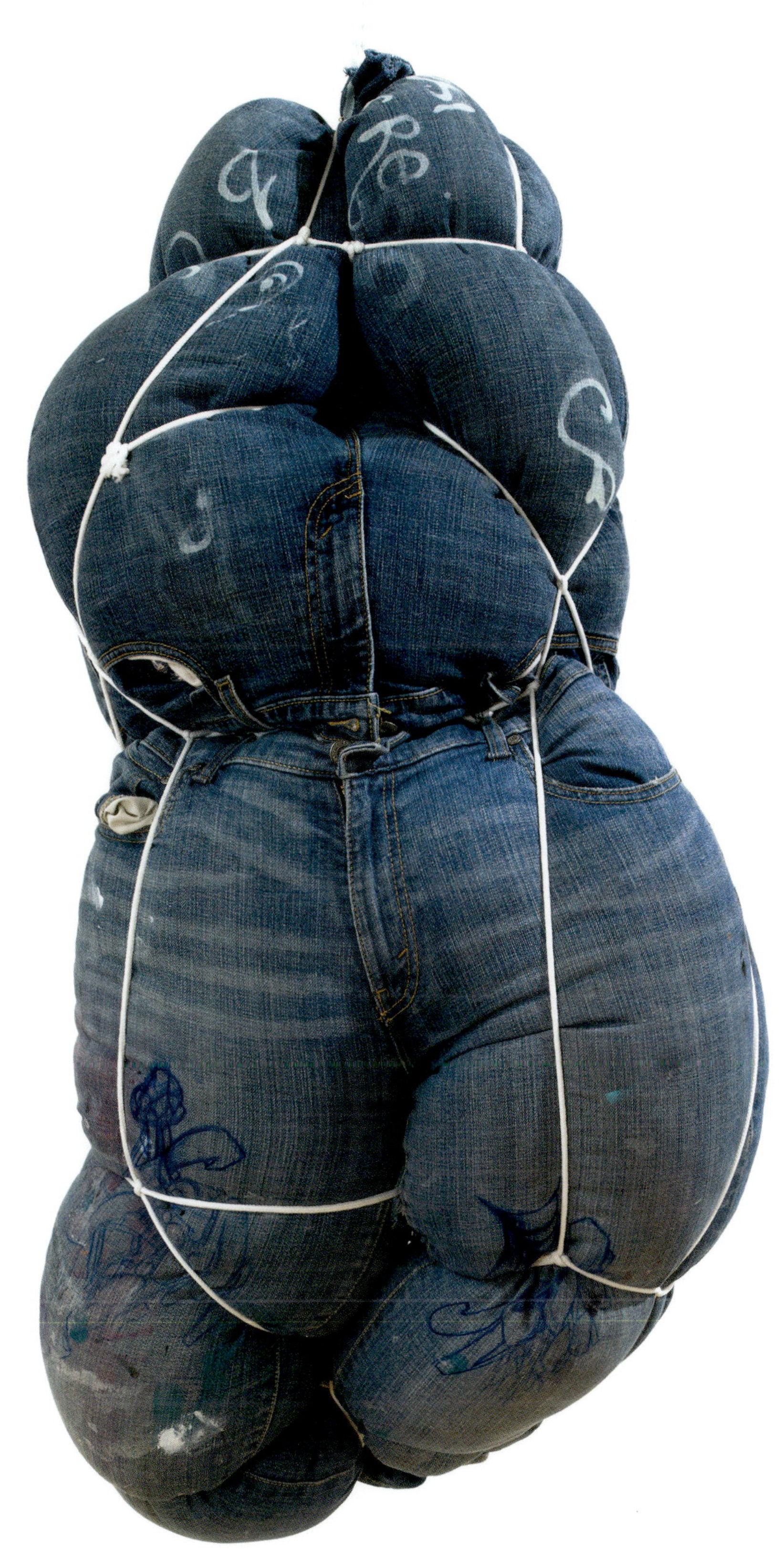

29   *Soul Elsewhere*
2013

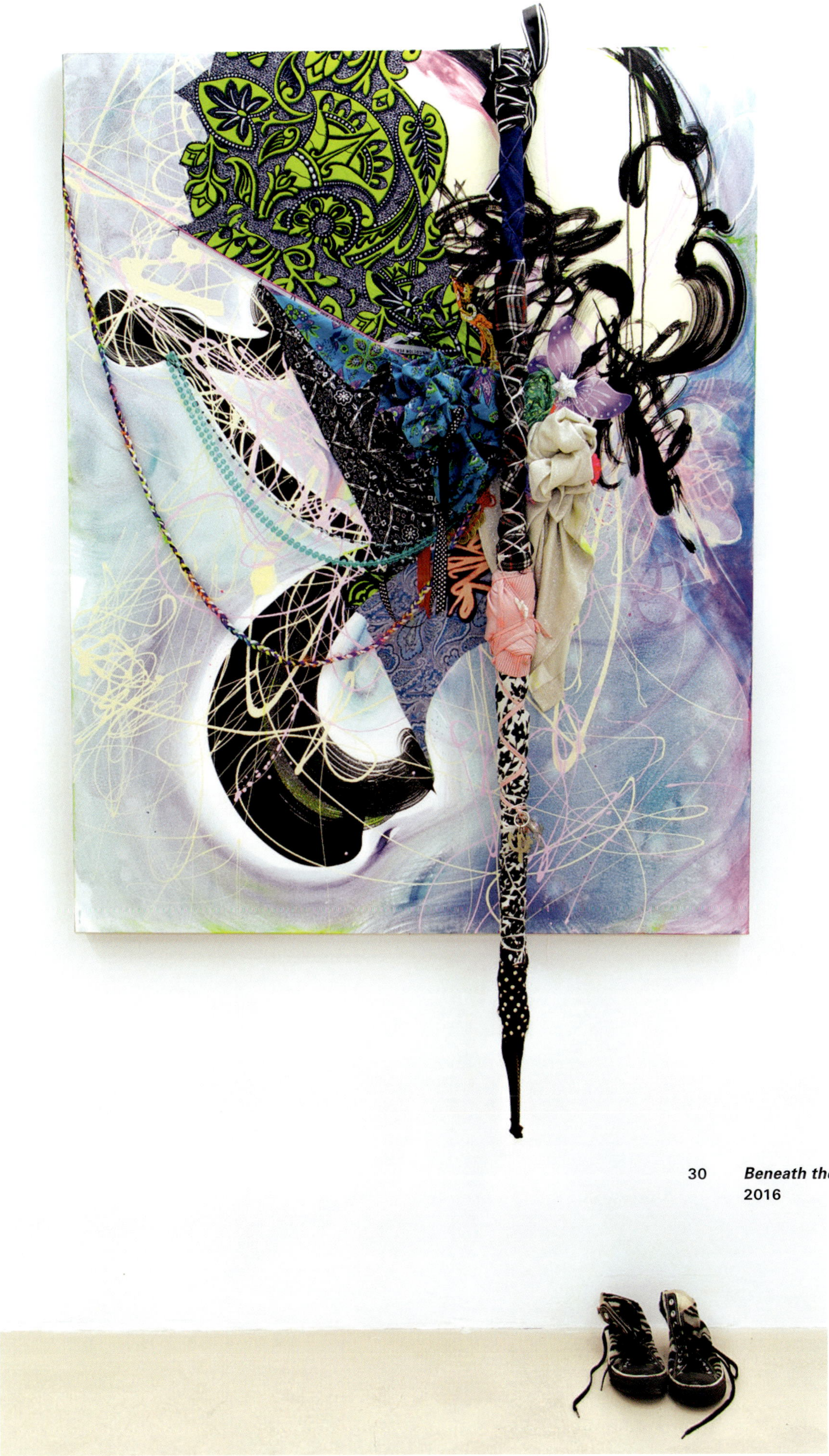

30   *Beneath the Blue Veil*
      2016

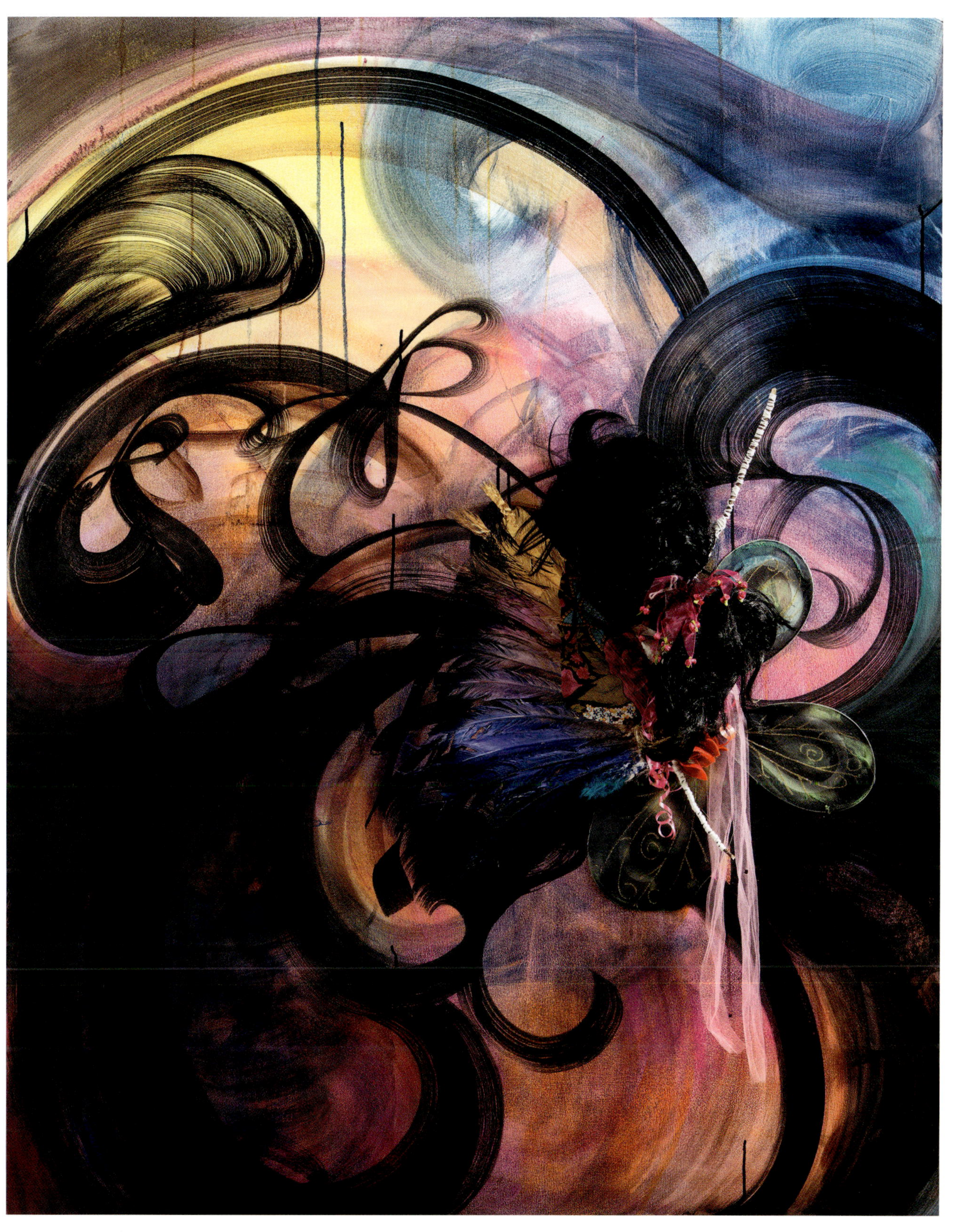

31 ***Ode to the StarSpun Seeker***
2012

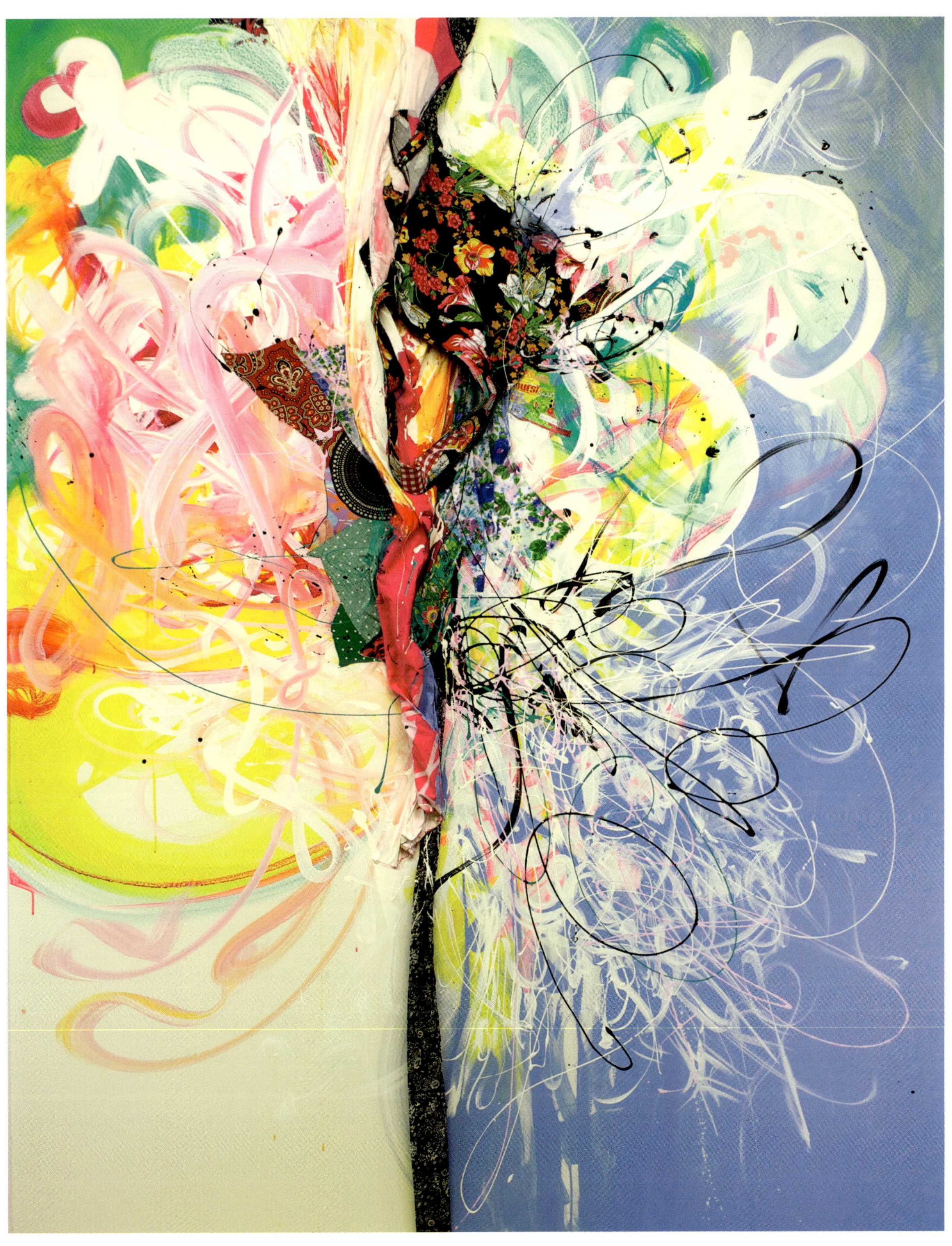

32   *Song thrown at the Sun*
2014

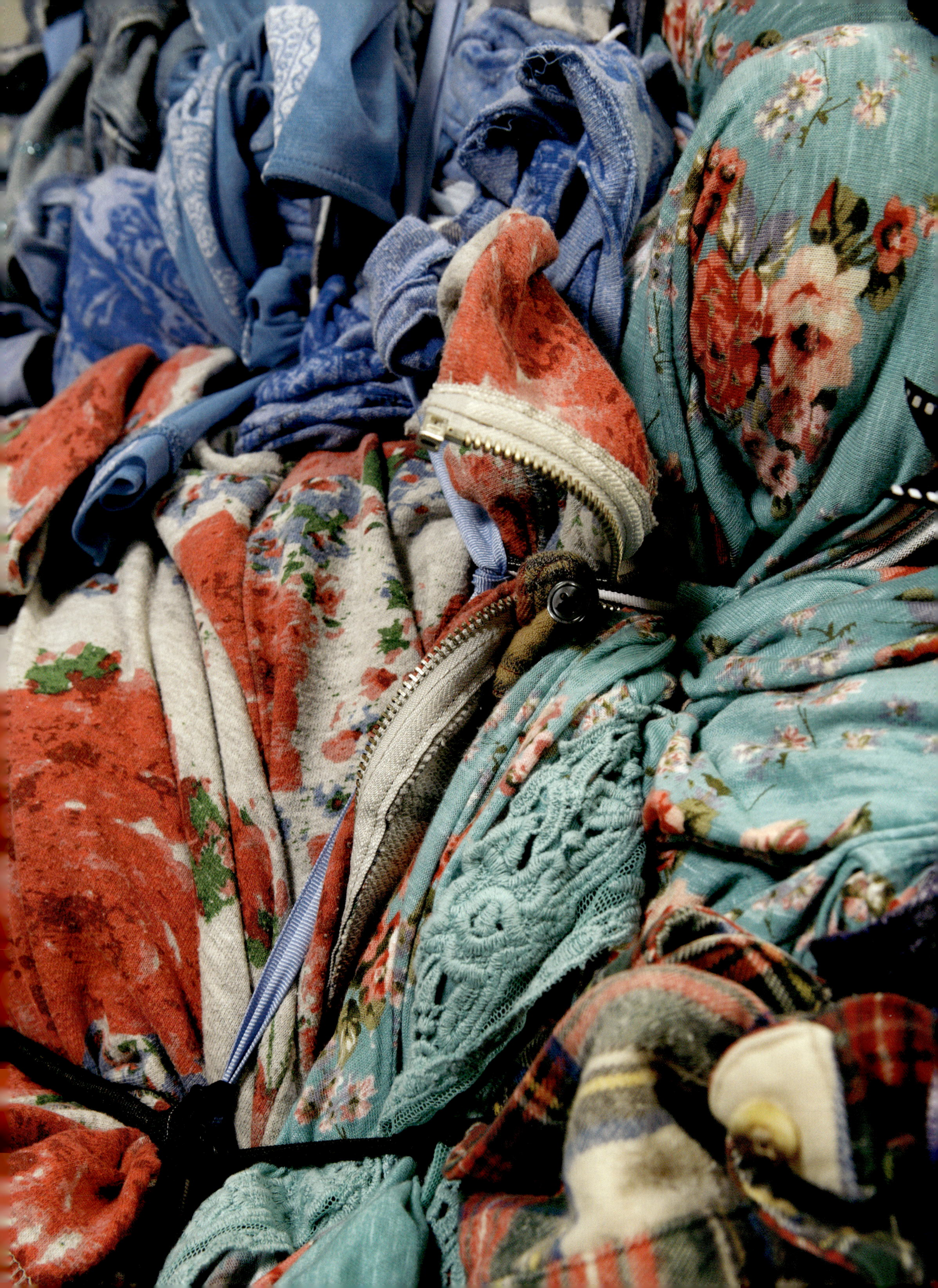

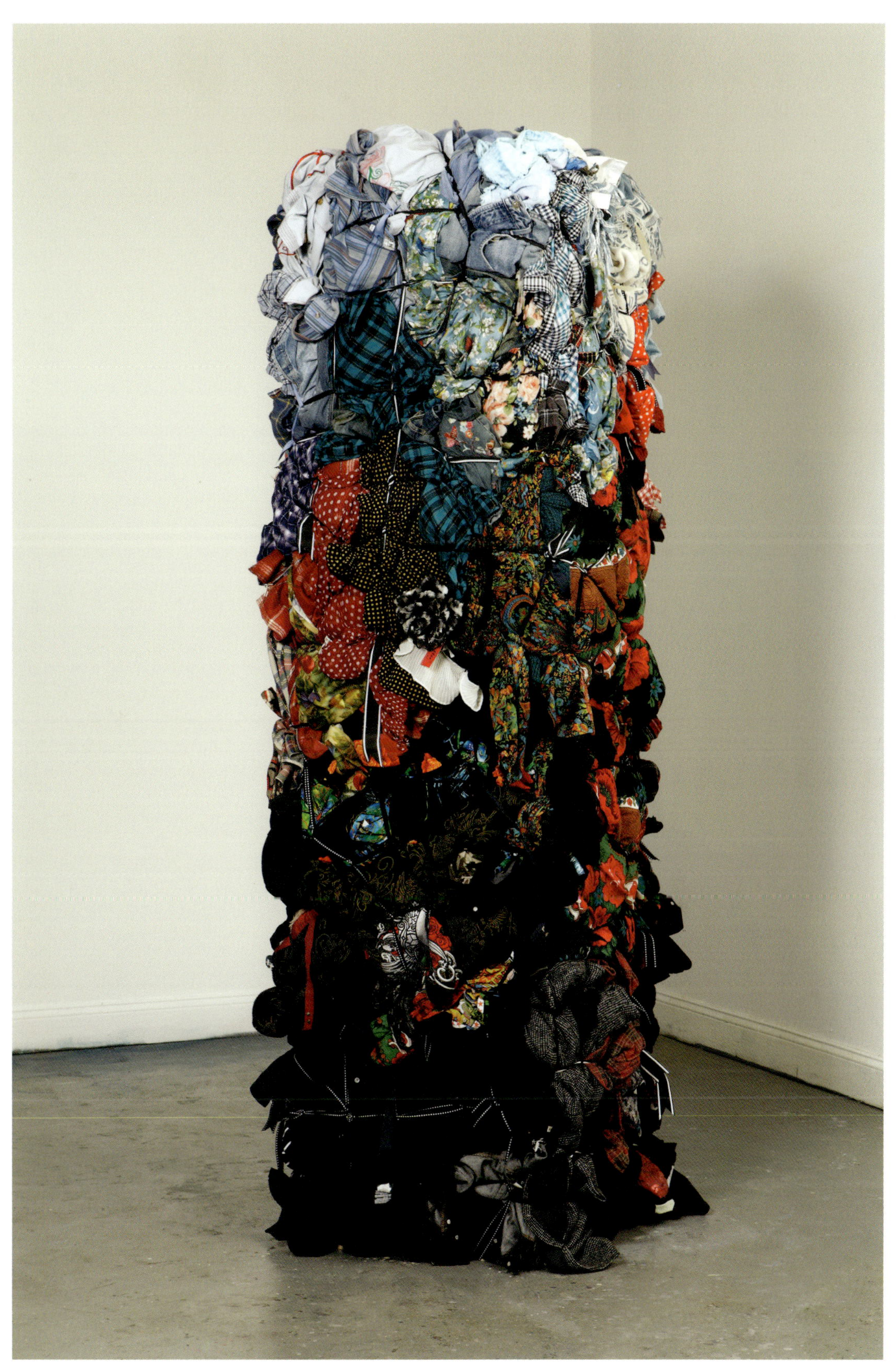

33   *Bale Variant No. 0022*
2012

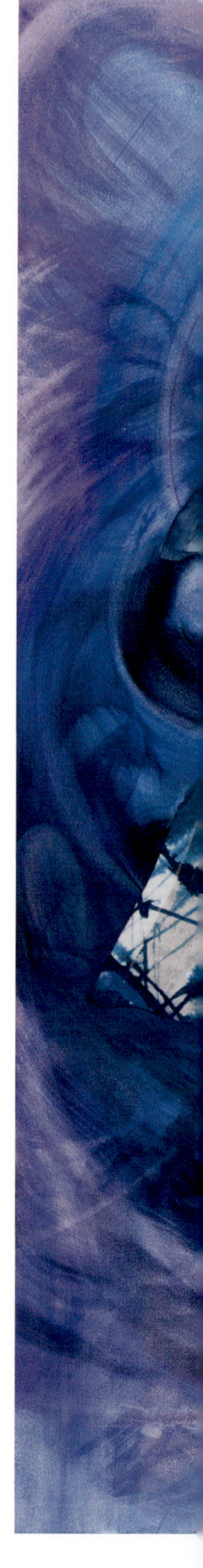

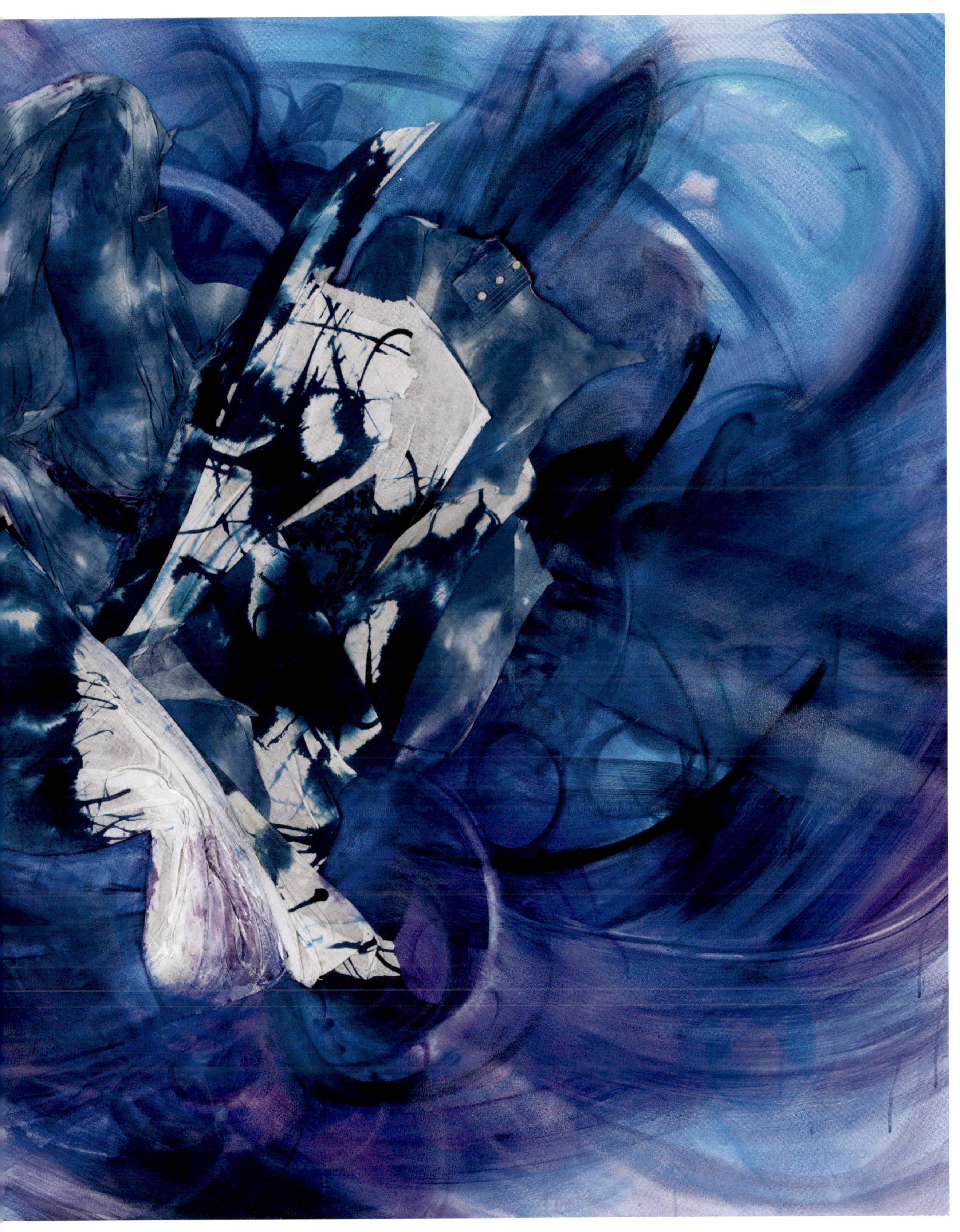

34   *The Oldest Love*
2013

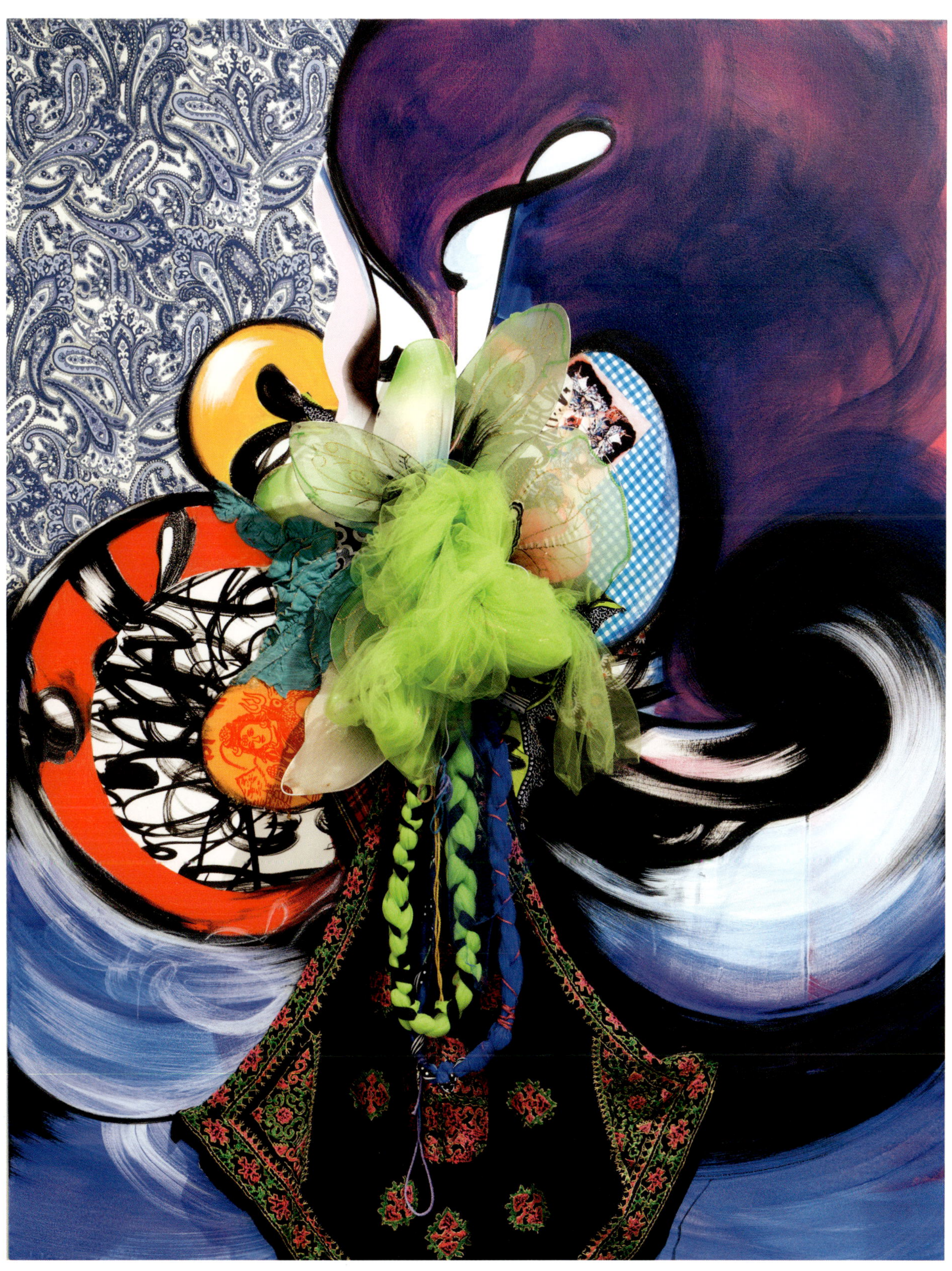

35   *Shield Maiden*
2014

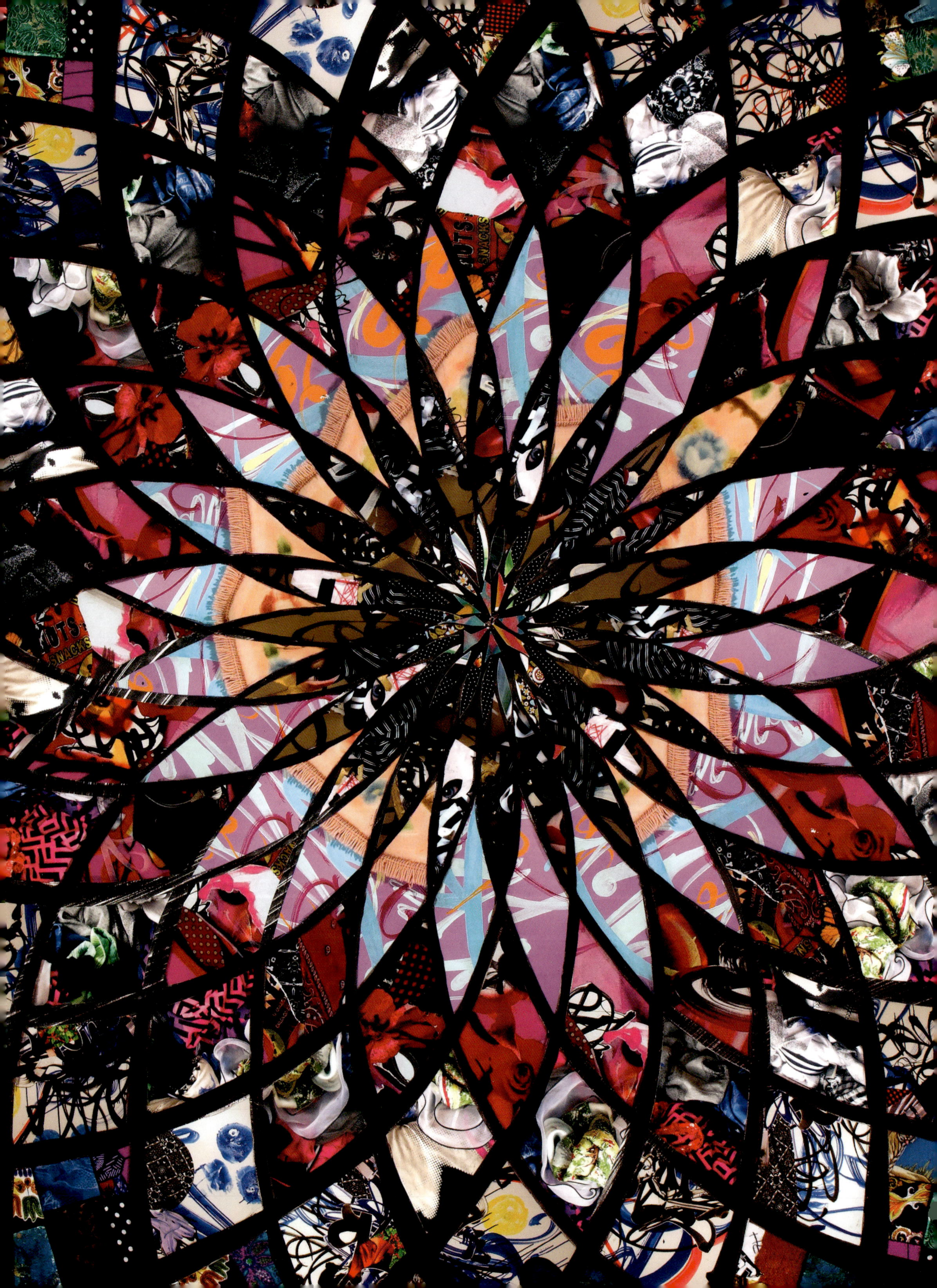

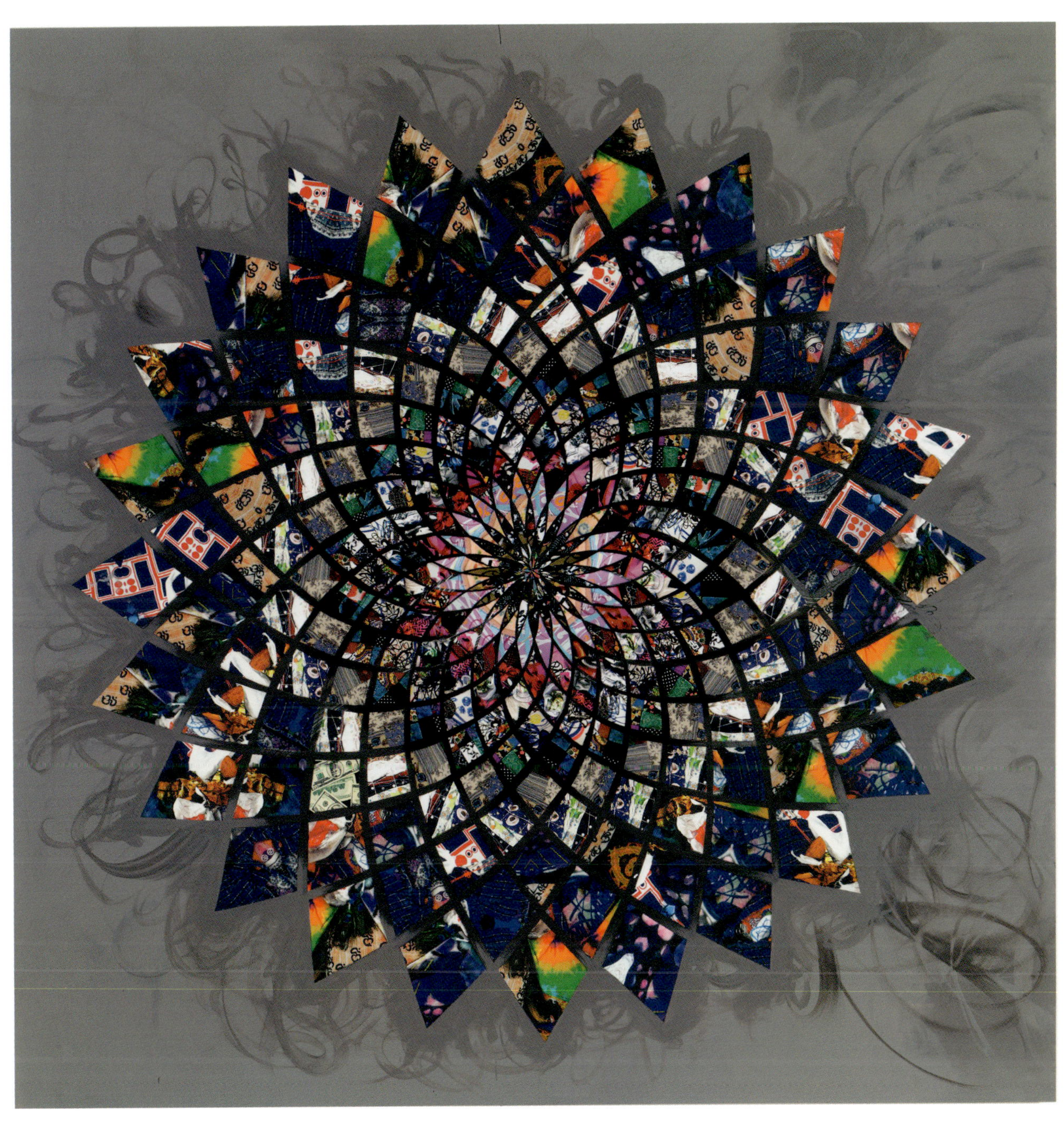

36   *My Song to Sing*
2013

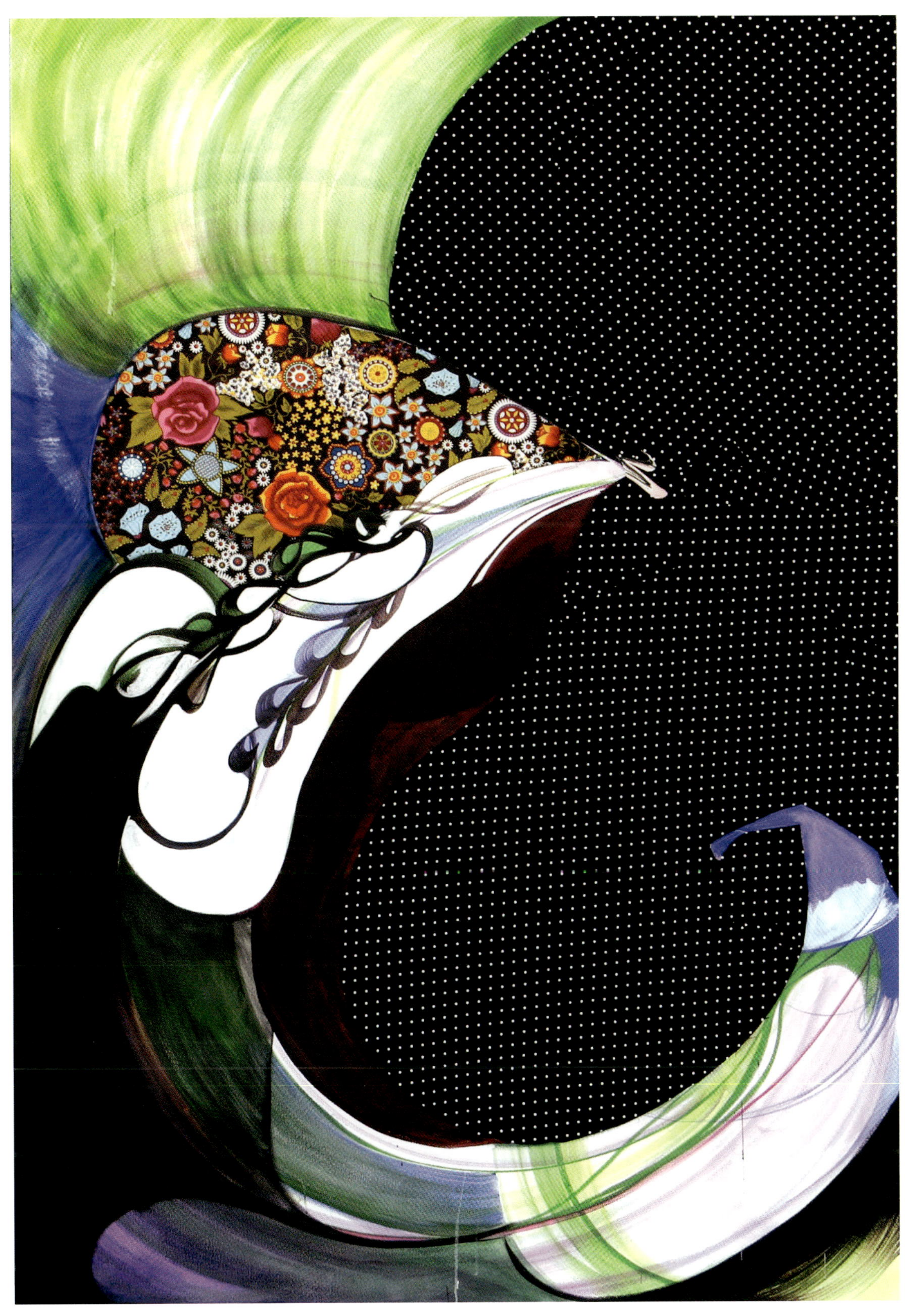

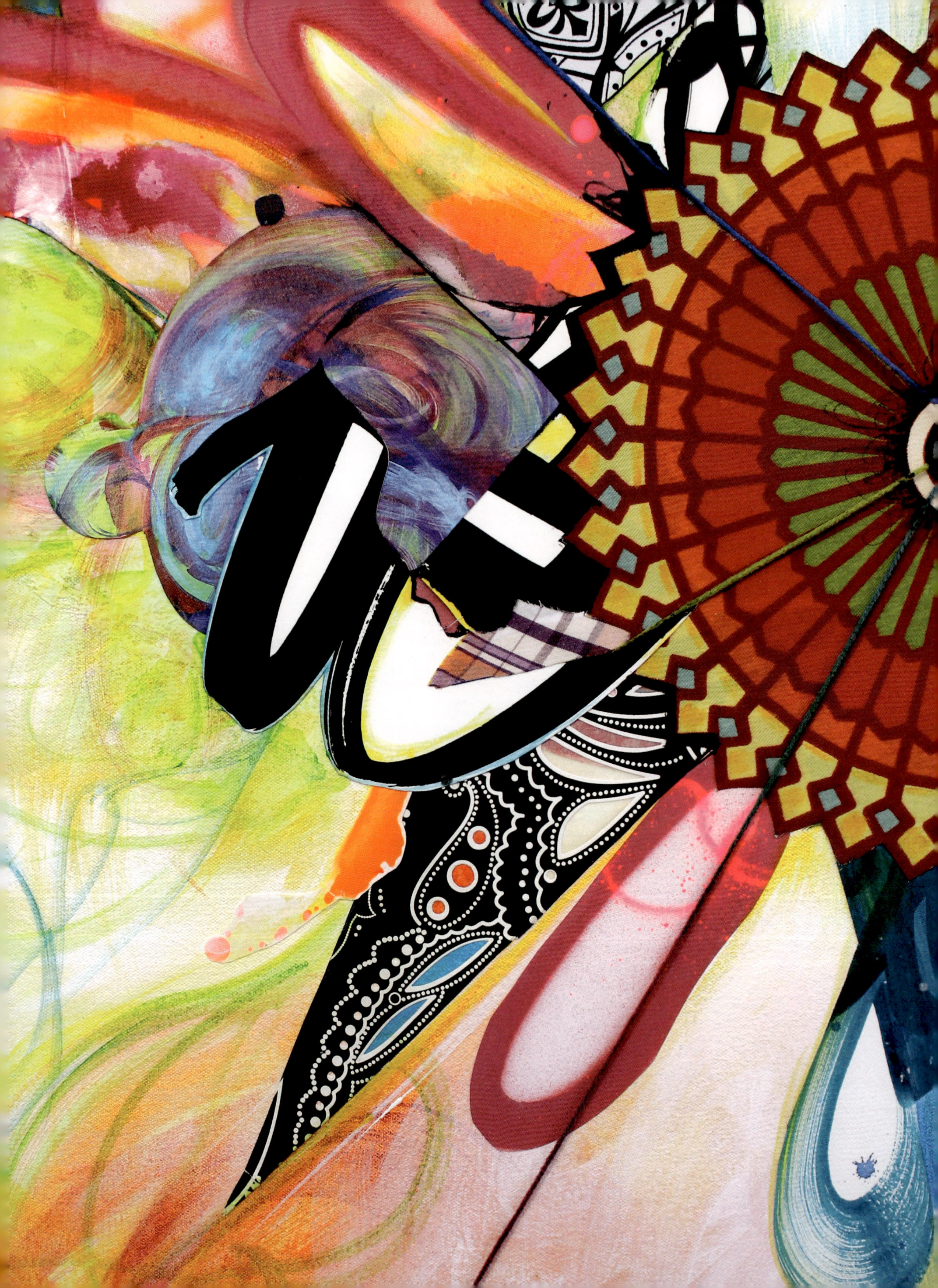

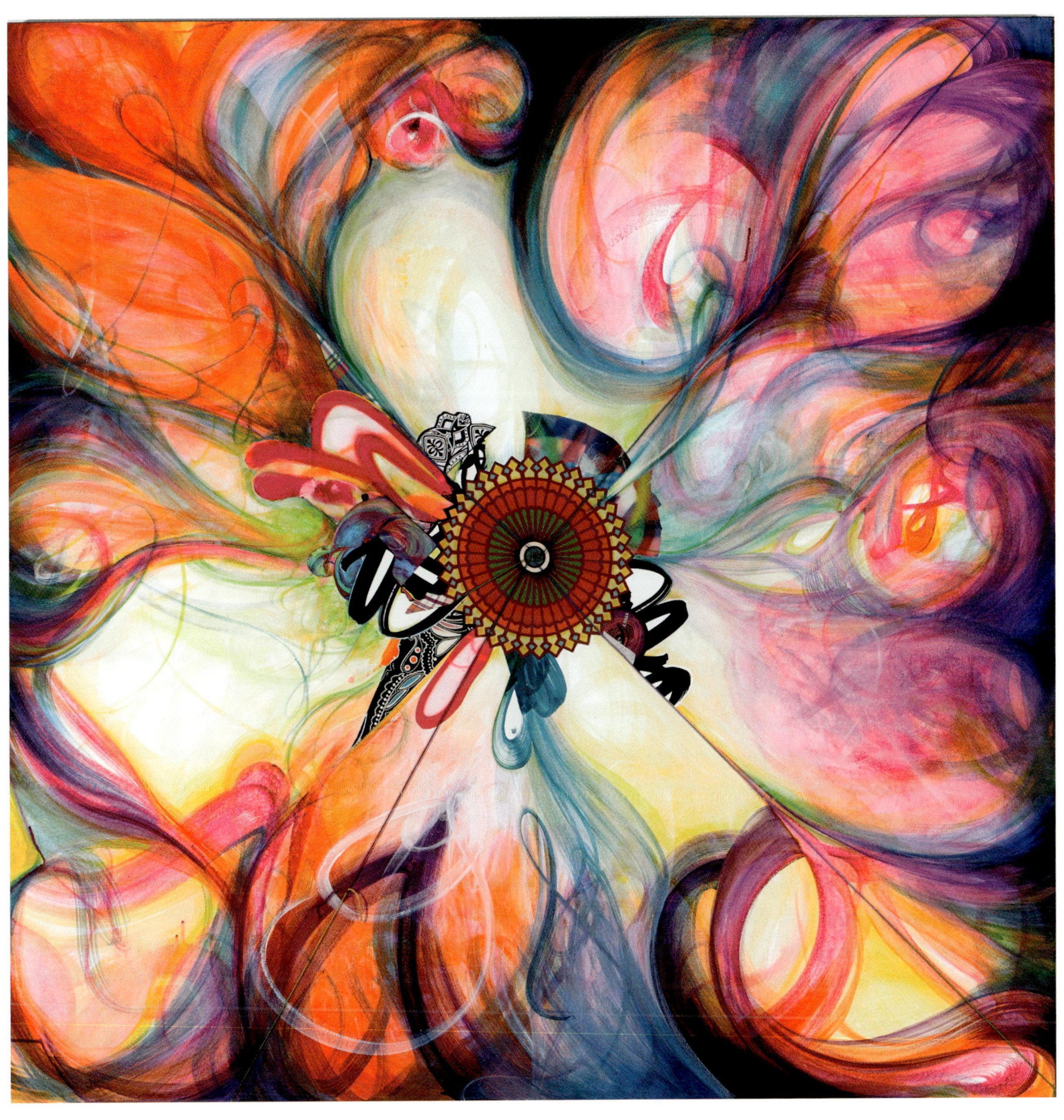

38 **_Always and Everywhere_**
2013

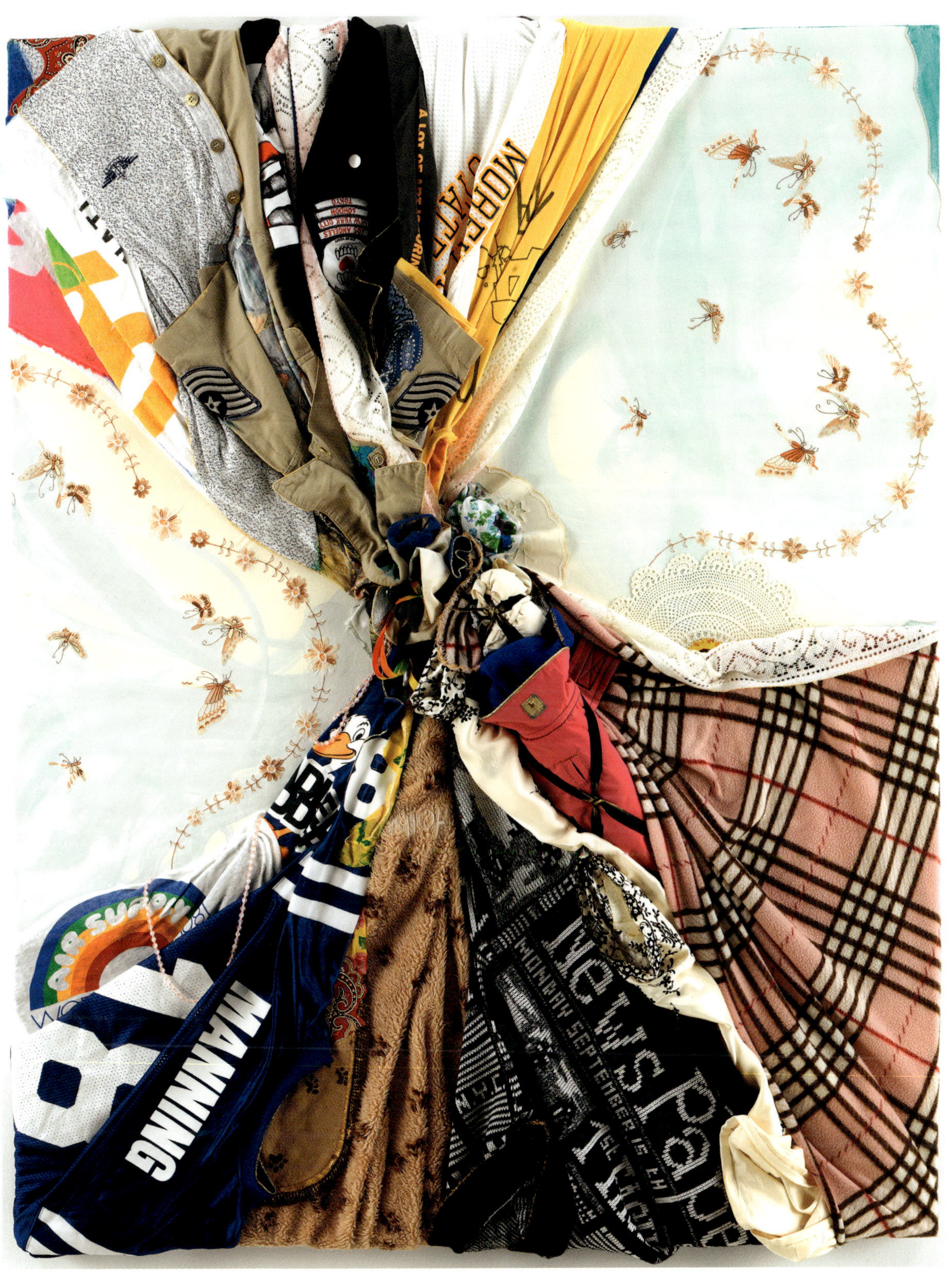

39   *The one that you love*
2015

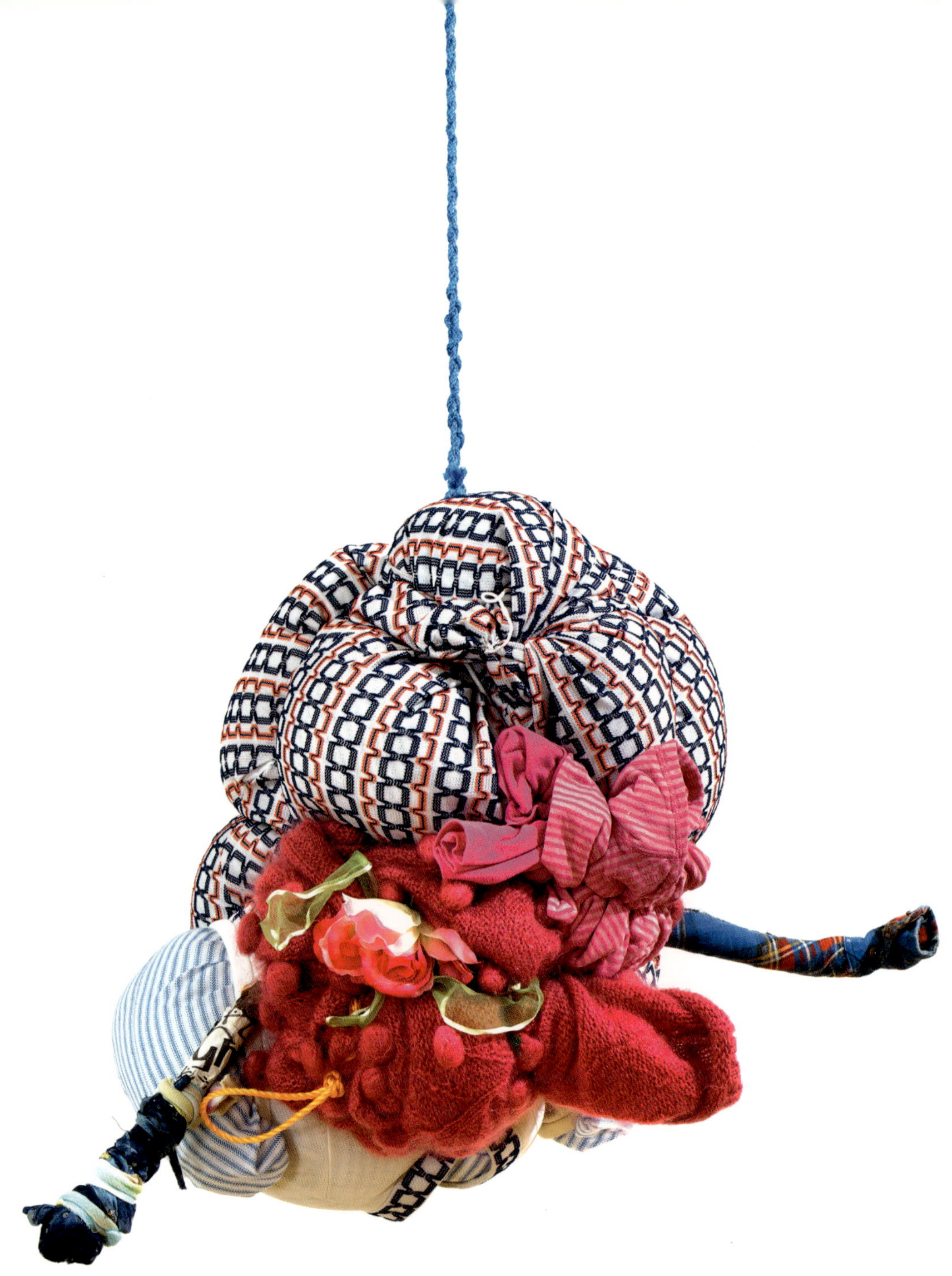

40   *Cathedral Street*
2013

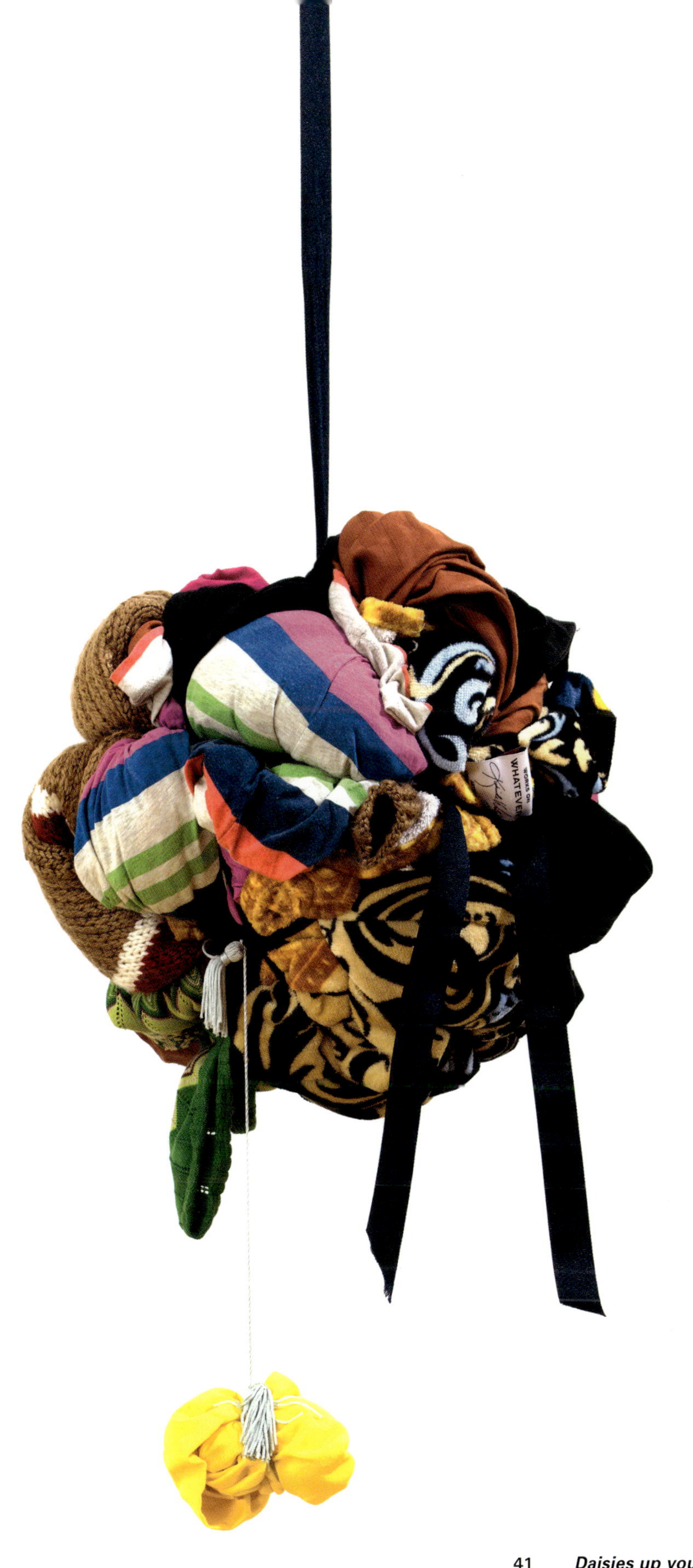

41   *Daisies up your butterfly*
2013

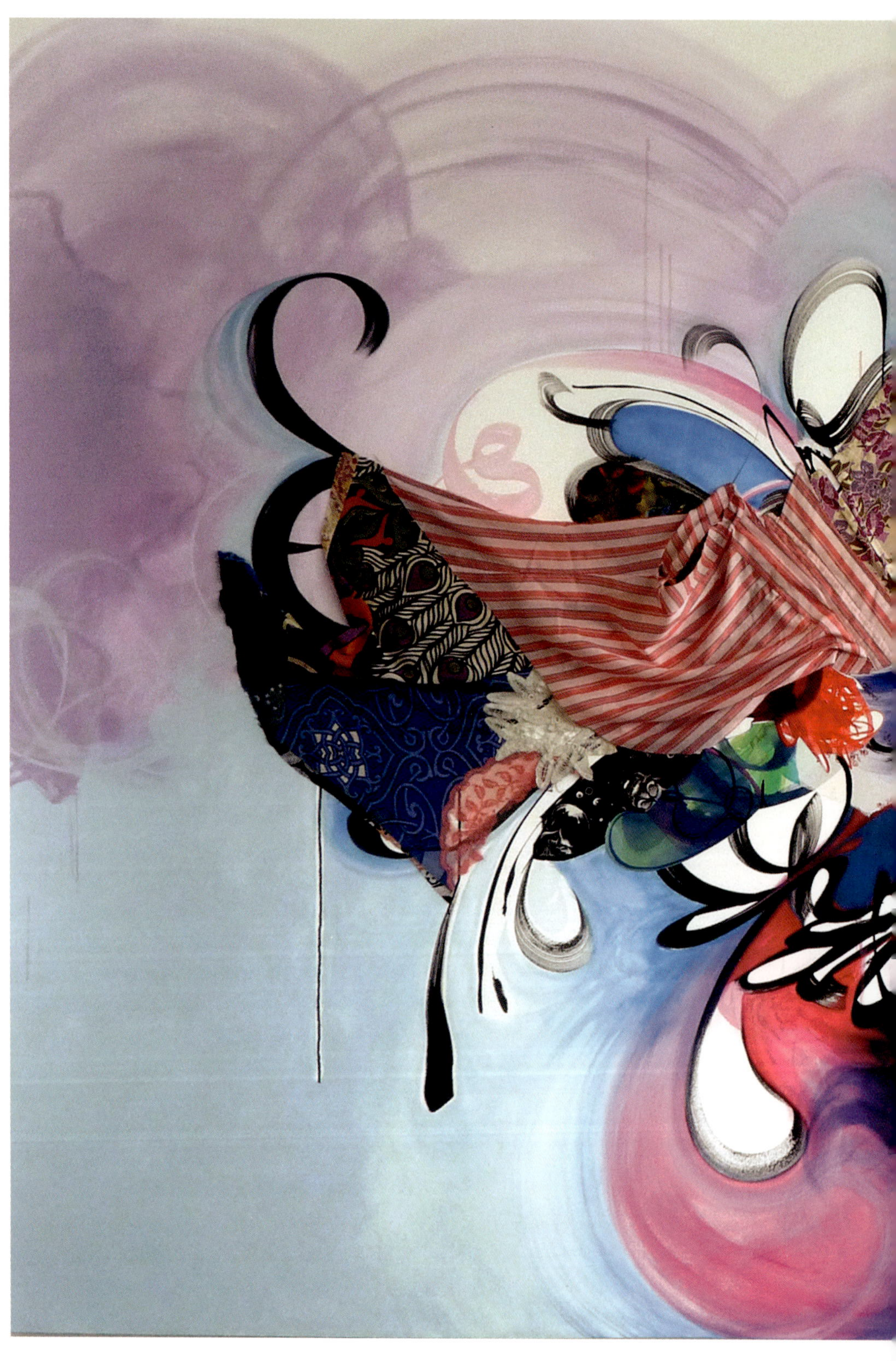

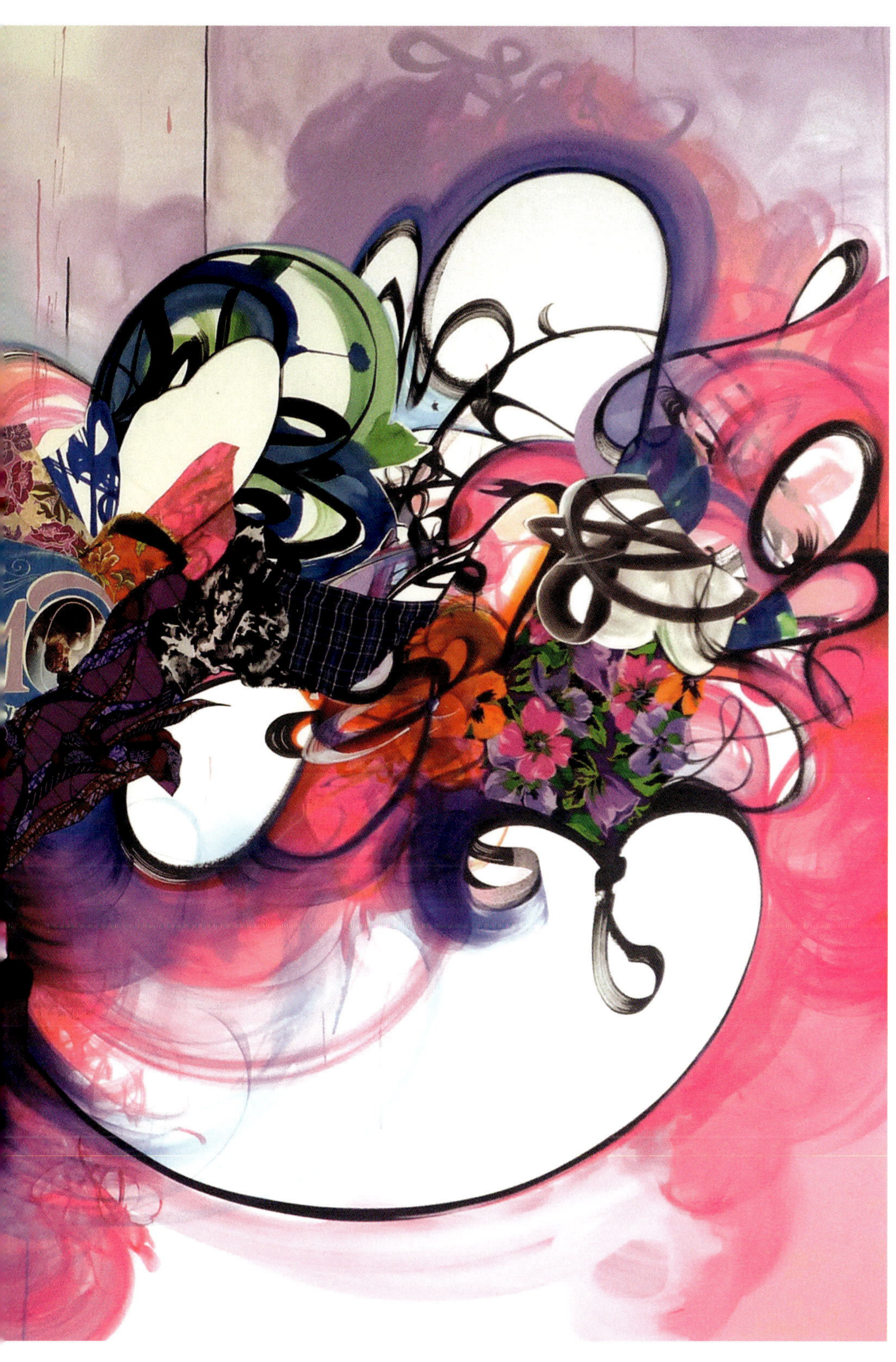

42 **Birdhouse of My Soul**
2011

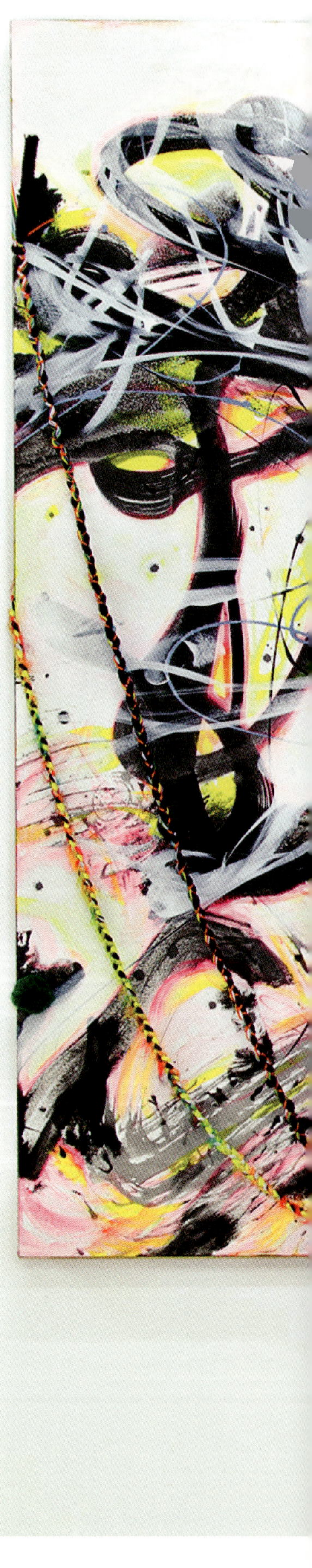

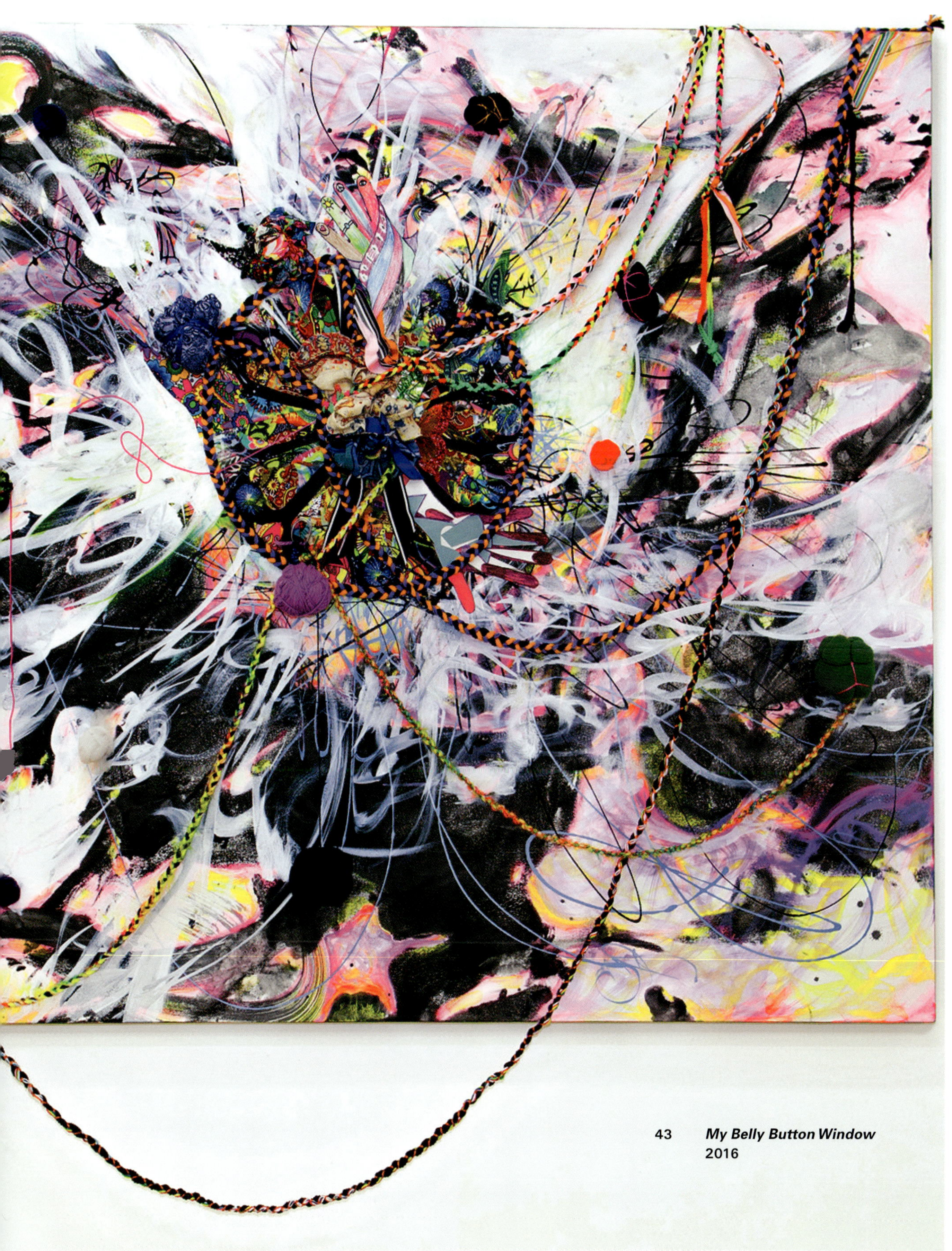

43   *My Belly Button Window*
2016

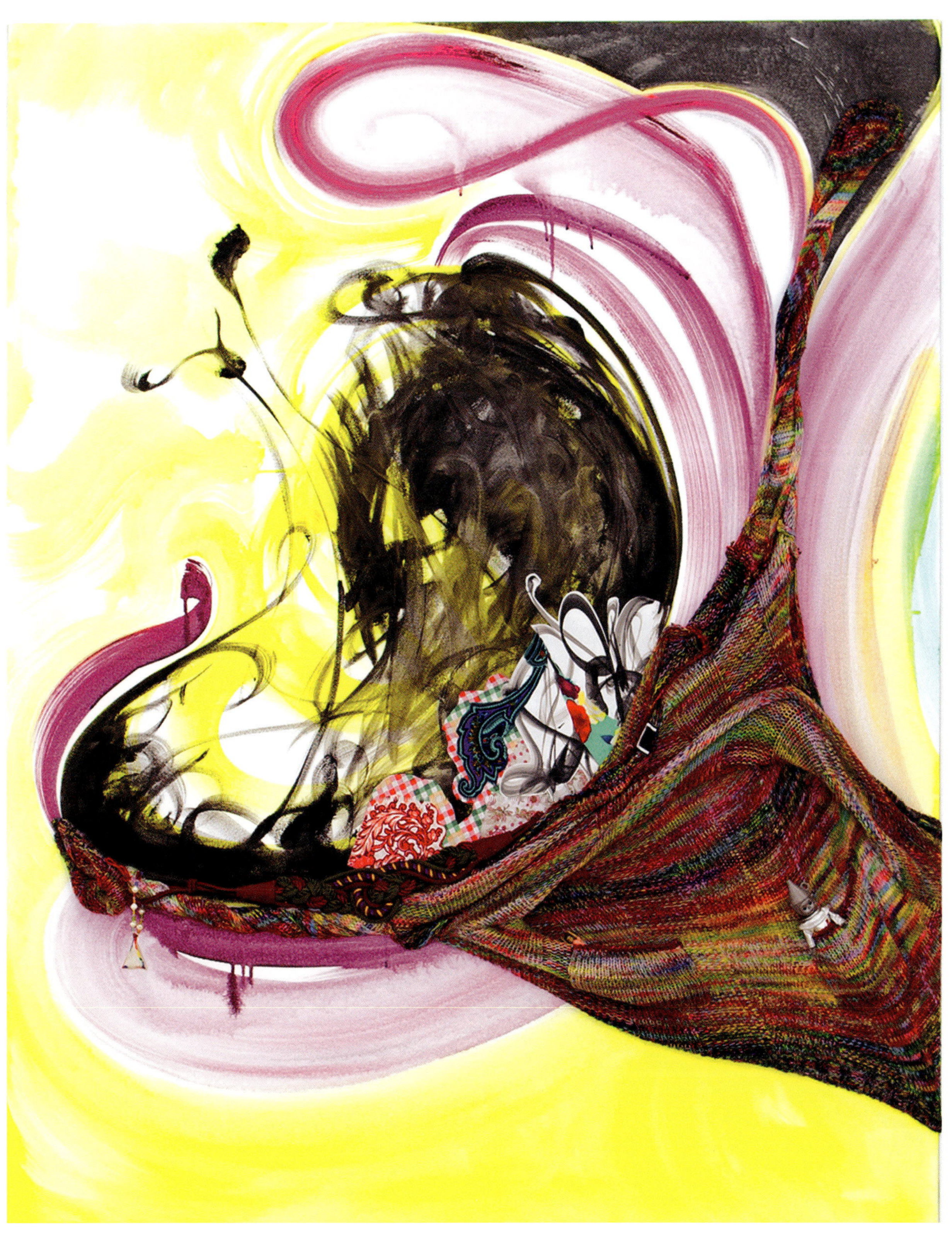

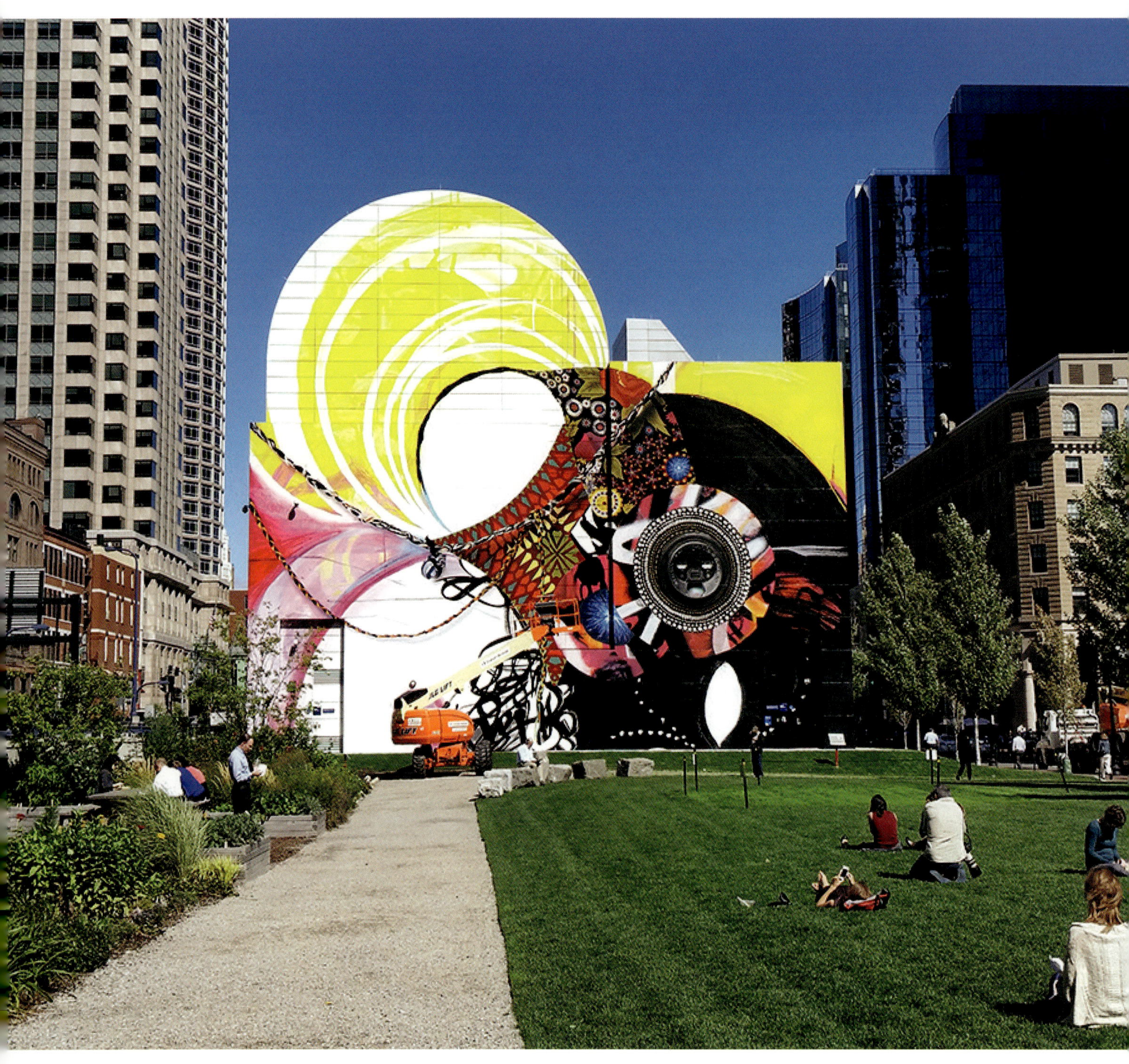

Shinique Smith (American, b. 1971). *Seven Moon Junction* (installation view, Dewey Square Park, Boston), 2014–15. Oil-based sign paint mural, 70 x 60 ft. Commissioned by the Rose Fitzgerald Kennedy Greenway Conservancy for the Greenway Wall, which exhibits temporary works by renowned artists annually

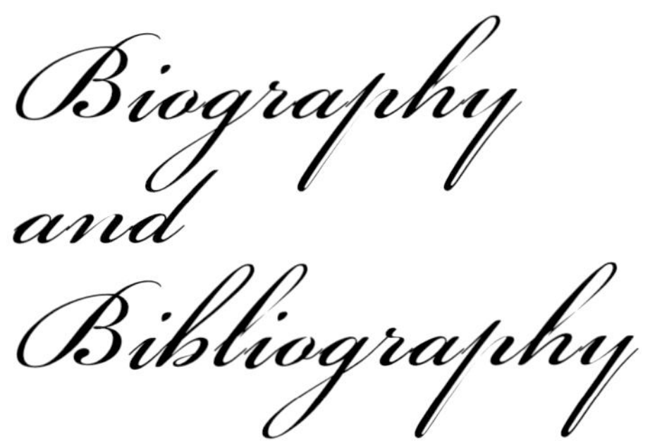

Biography and Bibliography

Shinique Smith

Born in 1971, Baltimore, Maryland
Lives and works in upstate New York

Education

2003
MFA, Maryland Institute College of Art
2000
MAT, Tufts University
1992
BFA, Maryland Institute College of Art

Selected Solo Exhibitions

2016
Shinique Smith: Quickening, Museum of
Contemporary Art, Project Atrium, Jacksonville,
Florida

2015
Mural exhibition, Aspen Art Museum at Elk
Camp, Aspen, Colorado
Shinique Smith: Wonder and Rainbows, Frist
Center for the Visual Arts, Nashville, Tennessee
Threaded, Center for the Arts at Virginia Tech,
Blacksburg, Virginia

2014
Shinique Smith: Bright Matter, Museum of Fine
Arts, Boston, Massachusetts
Shinique Smith: Changing Rooms, Galerie Henrik
Springmann, Berlin, Germany
Shinique Smith: Arcadian Clusters, Eli and
Edythe Broad Art Museum, East Lansing, Michigan

2013
Shinique Smith: Kaleidoscopic, David Castillo
Gallery, Miami, Florida
Shinique Smith: Bold As Love, James Cohan
Gallery, New York
Firsthand, Los Angeles County Museum of Art,
Los Angeles, California

2011
Shinique Smith: To the Ocean of Everyone Else,
Brand New Gallery, Milan, Italy
Shinique Smith: Urban Pastoral, Savannah College
of Art and Design (SCAD), Savannah, Georgia,
and SCAD Trois Gallery, Atlanta, Georgia
Shinique Smith: New Degree of Love, Galerie
Zidoun, Luxembourg City, Luxembourg
Shinique Smith: Menagerie, Madison Museum of
Contemporary Art, Madison, Wisconsin

2010
Shinique Smith: Every Brick, Southeastern
Center for Contemporary Art, Winston-Salem,
North Carolina
Shinique Smith: Menagerie, Museum of Contem-
porary Art, North Miami, Florida
Shinique Smith: No Words, Yvon Lambert, Paris,
France
Shinique Smith: My Heart Is My Hand, University
Galleries of Illinois State University, College of
Fine Arts, Normal, Illinois

2009

Ten Times Myself, Yvon Lambert, New York
Shinique Smith: Like it Like that, Studio Museum in Harlem, New York

2008

Good Knot, Yvon Lambert, London, England
Shinique Smith: Torch Songs, Saltworks Gallery, Atlanta, Georgia

2007

Shinique Smith: Lost & Found, Franklin Art Works, Minneapolis, Minnesota
Shinique Smith: Open Strings, Skestos Gabriele Gallery, Chicago, Illinois

2006

Shinique Smith: No dust, no stain, Cuchifritos Gallery and Project Space (Artists Alliance Inc.), New York

2005

Overstock, The Proposition, New York
FULL-ON!, Boulder Museum of Contemporary Art, Boulder, Colorado

Selected Group Exhibitions

2016

Revolution in the Making: Abstract Sculpture by Women, 1947–2016, Hauser, Wirth & Schimmel, Los Angeles, California

2015

Open Source (public art), Mural Arts, Philadelphia, Pennsylvania
To Be Young, Gifted, and Black, Goodman Gallery, Johannesburg, South Africa

2014

Between Critique and Absorption: Contemporary Art and Consumer Culture, Haggerty Museum of Art, Marquette University, Milwaukee, Wisconsin

2013

Outside the Lines, Contemporary Art Museum Houston, Houston, Texas
The Distaff Side, The Granary, Sharon, Connecticut
Etched in Collective History, Birmingham Art Museum, Birmingham, Alabama
Spun: Adventures in Textiles, Denver Art Museum, Denver, Colorado

2012

Dark Flow Lurking, David Castillo Gallery, Miami, Florida
Stretching the Limits: Fibers in Contemporary Painting, SCAD Museum of Art, Savannah, Georgia
Cultural Transference, Elizabeth Foundation for the Arts (EFA) Project Space, New York
Everyday Abstract—Abstract Everyday, James Cohan Gallery, New York
Flights from Wonder, Santa Barbara Contemporary Arts Forum, Santa Barbara, California

2011

The Bearden Project, Studio Museum in Harlem, New York
Don't Get High On Your Own Supply, David Castillo Gallery, Miami, Florida
Trash, New Children's Museum, San Diego, California
Play Time, Yvon Lambert, New York
Stargazers: Elizabeth Catlett in Conversation with 21 Contemporary Artists, Bronx Museum, New York

2010

THREADS: Textiles and Fiber in the Works of African American Artists, EK Projects, Beijing, China
Personal Freedom, Portugal Arte 10, Lisbon, Portugal
At Home/Not At Home: Works from the Collection of Martin and Rebecca Eisenberg, Hessel Museum of Art, Bard College, Annandale-on-Hudson, New York

2009

Extended Family: Contemporary Connections, Brooklyn Museum, New York
Embrace! Denver Art Museum, Denver, Colorado
30 Seconds off an Inch, Studio Museum in Harlem, New York
Into The Trees, The Fields Sculpture Park, Omi International Art Center, Ghent, New York

2008

30 Americans, Rubell Family Collection, Miami, Florida (traveled to: North Carolina Museum of Art, Raleigh, NC, 2011; Corcoran Gallery of Art, Washington, DC, 2011–12; Chrysler Museum of Art, Norfolk, VA, 2012; Milwaukee Art Museum, Milwaukee, WI, 2013; Frist Center for the Visual Arts, Nashville, TN, 2013–14; Contemporary Arts Center, New Orleans, LA, 2014; Arkansas Arts Center, Little Rock, AR, 2015; Detroit Institute of Arts, Detroit, MI, 2015–16; Cincinnati Art Museum, Cincinnati, OH, 2016)
Freeway Balconies, Deutsche Guggenheim, Berlin, Germany
Ready Made, Yvon Lambert, Paris, France
Waste Not, Want Not, Socrates Sculpture Park, Long Island City, New York
The Way That We Rhyme: Women, Art & Politics, Yerba Buena Center for the Arts, San Francisco, California

RECOGNIZE! Hip Hop and Contemporary Portraiture, National Portrait Gallery, Smithsonian Institution, Washington, DC
Something from Nothing, Contemporary Arts Center, New Orleans, Louisiana

2007

Unmonumental: The Object in the 21st Century, New Museum, New York
Body Politic: Casey Cook, Wangechi Mutu, Shinique Smith, Tory Wright, Branch Gallery, Durham, North Carolina
PrimeTime: Shinique Smith and Mickalene Thomas, Caren Golden Gallery, New York
Future Nomad, Vox Populi, Philadelphia, Pennsylvania

2006

Altered, Stitched and Gathered, P.S.1 Contemporary Art Center, New York
Allegories of Displacement, Westport Arts Center, Westport, Connecticut
I Feel You, Roebling Hall, Williamsburg (Brooklyn), New York

2005

Frequency, Studio Museum in Harlem, New York
Two Continents and Beyond: Waterways, 9th International Istanbul Biennial, Istanbul, Turkey
Unveiling the Invisible: Contemporary Video Art (Desvelar lo invisible: Videocreación contemporánea), Comunidad de Madrid, Madrid, Spain
Recess, Rush Arts Gallery, New York
African Queen, Studio Museum in Harlem, New York

2004
Re: Source, Art in General, New York
The Reality of Things, Triple Candie, New York
Veni Vidi Video II, Studio Museum in Harlem,
New York
Super Salon, Samson Projects, Boston, Massachusetts

Permanent Collections

Ackland Art Museum, University of North
Carolina at Chapel Hill
Brooklyn Museum
Denver Art Museum
Los Angeles County Museum of Art
Margulies Collection at the Warehouse, Miami
Metropolitan Transportation Authority | Arts for
Transit, New York City
Museum of Contemporary Art, North Miami
Museum of Fine Arts, Boston
Palmer Museum of Art at Penn State University
Rubell Family Collection, Miami
Studio Museum in Harlem, New York
Whitney Museum of American Art, New York

Residencies, Fellowships, and Awards

Louis Comfort Tiffany Foundation Biennial
Award, 2013
Alumni Medal of Honor, Maryland Institute
College of Art, 2012
Joan Mitchell Foundation Fellowship, 2008
New York Foundation for the Arts, Gregory
Millard Fellowship in Sculpture, 2007
Headlands Center for the Arts, Artist-in-Residence,
2007
Aljira, a Center for Contemporary Art, Fellowship,
2005
Henry Street Settlement, Artist-in-Residence,
2005
Lower Manhattan Cultural Council, Studio
Residency, 2003
Skowhegan School of Painting & Sculpture,
Fellowship, 2003
Vermont Studio Center, Fellowship, 2002

Selected Publications

*Revolution in the Making: Abstract Sculpture by
Women, 1947–2016*. Edited by Paul Schimmel
and Jenni Sorkin. New York: Skira Rizzoli, 2016.

Feelings: Soft Art. Contributions by John Baldessari, Simon Castets, Tracey Emin, Ryan McGinley,
and Sarah Nicole Prickett. New York: Skira Rizzoli,
2015.

The Distaff Side. Contributions by Melva Bucksbaum, Ryan Frank, Steven Learner, Raymond
Learsy, Joan Simon, Caitlin Smith, and Elisabeth
Sussman. Sharon, CT: Granary, 2014.

*New York's Underground Art Museum: MTA Arts
and Design*. Sandra Bloodworth and William
Ayres. Foreword by Stanley Tucci. Preface by
Thomas F. Prendergast. New York: Monacelli
Press, 2013.

Shinique Smith: To the Ocean of Everyone Else.
Brian Keith Jackson. Milan, Italy: Brand New
Gallery, 2011.

Stargazers. Foreword by Holly Block. Essays by Isolde Brielmaier, Xaviera Simmons, and Franklin Sirmans. Interview with Elizabeth Catlett by Emma Amos. New York: Bronx Museum, 2011.

At Home/Not At Home: Works from the Collection of Martin and Rebecca Eisenberg. Edited by Matthew Higgs. Annandale-on-Hudson, NY: CCS Bard Hessel Museum, 2010.

Shinique Smith: Menagerie. Essays by Bonnie Clearwater, Paul D. Miller, and Jane Simon. North Miami: Museum of Contemporary Art, 2010.

Embrace! Edited by Gwen Chanzit. Denver: Denver Art Museum, 2009.

30 Americans. Contributions by Robert Hobbs, Glenn Ligon, Franklin Sirmans, and Michele Wallace. Miami: Rubell Family Collection, 2008.

Freeway Balconies. Contributions by Dominic Eichler, Sarah Lewis, Collier Schorr, and Nancy Spector. Berlin: Deutsche Guggenheim, 2008.

Unmonumental: The Object in the 21st Century. Richard Flood, Massimiliano Gioni, Laura Hoptman, and Trevor Smith. New York: New Museum and Phaidon Press, 2007.

Frequency. Ali Evans, Malik Gaines, Thelma Golden, Christine Y. Kim, and Franklin Sirmans. New York: Studio Museum in Harlem, 2005.

Unveiling the Invisible: Contemporary Video Art. Victòria Combalia and Juan Carlos Rego. Madrid: Comunidad de Madrid, 2005.

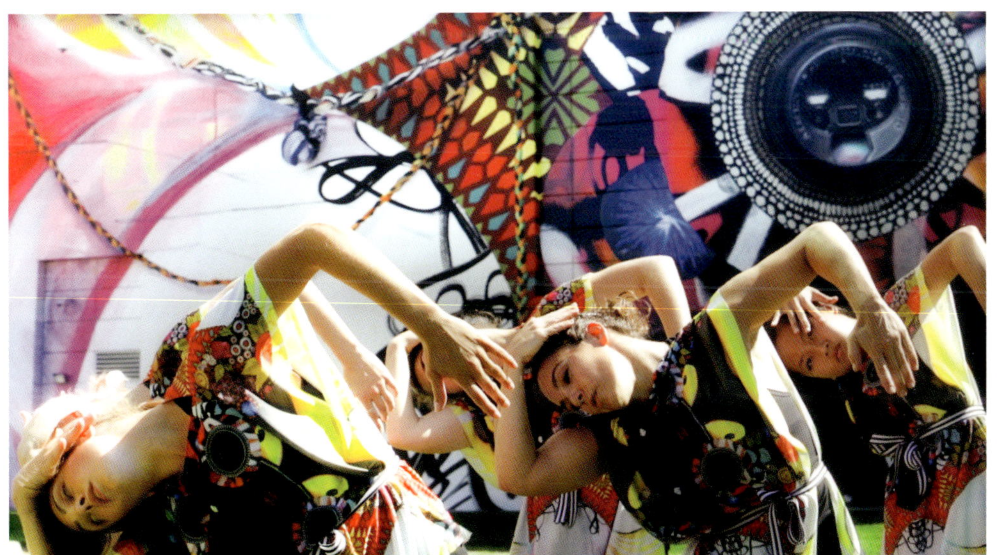

Shinique Smith. *Gesture III: One Great Turning* (still), 2015. Digital video created by Smith with Gary Pennock, in collaboration with KAIROS Dance Theater. Commissioned by the Rose Fitzgerald Kennedy Greenway Conservancy, Boston

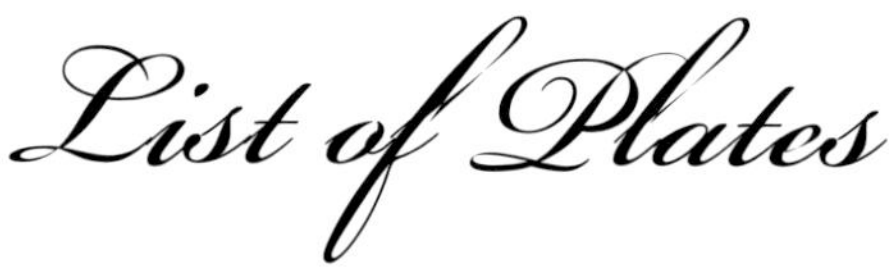

List of Plates

1. *Inner Clock*, 2014
Acrylic, ink, fabric, paper collage, and found objects on wood panel
64 x 48 x 8 in.
Courtesy of the artist and David Castillo Gallery, Miami

2. *Somewhere out there (in here)*, 2011
Ink, acrylic, and fabric collage on canvas over wood panel
Diptych: 60 x 96 x 2 in. overall
Private collection, New York

3. *Tiny Dancer*, 2013
Acrylic, fabric, collage, and slipper on canvas over wood panel
60 x 60 x 3 1/2 in.
Collection of Elizabeth Dascal, Miami

4. *Angel*, 2011
Clothing, fabric, acrylic spray paint, bleach, ribbon, rope, and found objects
25 x 16 x 15 in.
Collection of the artist

5. *Tongues became flowers*, 2013
Artist's clothing, fabric, Poly-Fil, ribbon, and rope
Approx. 30 x 24 x 19 in.
Collection of Christopher Dlutowski and Peter Occolowitz

6. *Black Cluster*, 2015
Clothing, ribbon, rope, beanbag chair, and car fresheners
Approx. 28 x 24 x 24 in.
Courtesy of the artist and David Castillo Gallery, Miami

7. *When Shadows Fall (Home)*, 2014
Ink, acrylic, fabric, collage, and found objects on canvas over wood panel
84 x 60 x 2 1/2 in.
Courtesy of the artist and David Castillo Gallery, Miami

8. *Open Word Lattice (Black & Rainbow)*, 2015
Ink, acrylic, fabric, and collage on cut wood
60 x 52 x 52 in.
Private collection, Nashville

9. *By the Light*, 2013
Ink, acrylic, fabric, and paper collage on canvas over wood panel
84 x 60 x 6 in.
Collection of Francie Bishop Good and David Horvitz

10. *Forever Strong*, 2014
Ink, acrylic, fabric, vintage hubcap, and ribbon collage on canvas over wood panel
60 x 60 x 5 1/2 in.
Private collection, Miami

11. *Gifted*, 2014
Ink, acrylic, paper, fabric collage, and found objects on canvas over wood panel
84 x 60 x 6 in.
Private collection, Caracas

12. *Day/Night*, 2011–13
Ink, acrylic, fabric, and paper collage on canvas
Diptych: 24 x 36 x 2 in. overall
Collection of Christopher Dlutowski and Peter Occolowitz

13. *Hammer*, 2013
Clothing, fabric, ink and dye, bamboo, ribbon,
and rope
44 x 22 x 12 in.
Courtesy of the artist and David Castillo Gallery,
Miami

14. *Dusk*, 2012
Clothing, fabric, ribbon, and acrylic on wood
panel
48 x 60 x 4 in.
Courtesy of the artist and David Castillo Gallery,
Miami

15. *Black/Blue/Green/Yellow/Orange/
Red/Pink*, 2015
Clothing, fabric, and ribbon on wood panel
196 x 72 x 6 in.
Courtesy of the artist and David Castillo Gallery,
Miami

16. *Bright Matter*, 2013
Clothing, fabric, and ribbon on wood panel
63 x 52 x 5 in.
Zang Collection, London

17. *Right through You*, 2014
Ink, acrylic, fabric, ribbon, and collage on wood
panel
60 x 48 x 2 in.
Zang Collection, London

18. *Of a Particular Perfume*, 2011
Acrylic, ink, crocheted shawl, fabric, and found
felt bunny on wood panel
60 x 96 x 2 1/2 in.
Private collection, Miami

19. *No Key, No Question*, 2013
Ink, acrylic, fabric, and collage on canvas over
panel
48 x 48 x 2 in.
The Pamela Joyner/Fred Giuffrida Collection

20. *Splendid*, 2014
Ink, acrylic, fabric, paper collage, yarn, ribbon,
beads, and bundled fabric on wood panel
60 x 78 x 6 in.
Museum of Fine Arts, Boston. Museum purchase
with funds donated by Barbara Karp Shuster
through The Heritage Fund for a Diverse Collection in memory of her mother, Mrs. Harold Karp.
2015.1

21. *Bale Variant No. 0023 (Totem)*, 2014
Clothing, fabric, accessories, twine, and wood
96 x 18 x 18 in.
Courtesy of the artist and David Castillo Gallery,
Miami

22. *The Power to See*, 2012
Ink, acrylic, fabric, collage, costume wings, and
paper on canvas over wood panel
84 x 120 x 4 in.
Collection of Jacqueline Brady and Clarence Otis

23. *With wings, newly made of water*,
2014
Ink, acrylic, fabric, collage, braided ribbon, yarn,
and beads on wood panel
60 x 48 x 3 in.
Private collection

24. *This Yellow Shell*, 2013
Clothing, fabric, bamboo, ribbon, rope,
and twine
65 x 15 1/2 x 12 in.
Zang Collection, London

25. *Seven Moons*, 2013
Ink, acrylic, fabric, paper collage, spray paint,
and coffee cup lid on canvas over wood panel
60 x 48 x 3 in.
Private collection, Miami

26. *Majesty*, 2012
Ink and acrylic on canvas over panel
96 x 120 x 2 in.
The Pamela Joyner/Fred Giuffrida Collection

27. *Gravity of Love*, 2013
Ink, acrylic, paper, and fabric collage on
wood panel
84 x 84 x 2 1/4 in.
Brooklyn Museum, Alfred T. White Fund,
2013.29.1

28. *Through native streets*, 2011
Ink, acrylic, fabric, paper collage, and found
objects on canvas over wood panel
60 x 48 x 6 in.
Collection of the artist

29. *Soul Elsewhere*, 2013
Artist's denim jeans, bleach, ink, fiberfill, and rope
56 x 18 x 12 in.
Private collection

30. *Beneath the Blue Veil*, 2016
Ink, acrylic, fabric, collage, ribbon, yarn,
and objects
70 x 48 x 6 in.
Courtesy of the artist and David Castillo Gallery,
Miami

31. *Ode to the StarSpun Seeker*, 2012
Ink, acrylic, fabric, collage, wig, ribbon, feathers,
and found objects on canvas over wood panel
60 x 48 x 7 in.
Private collection, Germany

32. *Song thrown at the Sun*, 2014
Ink, acrylic, fabric, and collage on wood panel
78 x 60 x 5 in.
Courtesy of the artist and David Castillo Gallery,
Miami

33. *Bale Variant No. 0022*, 2012
Clothing, fabric, ribbon, twine, and wood
90 x 30 x 30 in.
Collection of Jack and Sandra Guthman

34. *The Oldest Love*, 2013
Ink, acrylic, fabric, and collage on canvas over
wood panel
60 x 60 x 2 1/2 in.
Private collection, Houston

35. *Shield Maiden*, 2014
Ink, acrylic, fabric, and collage
60 x 48 x 9 in.
Courtesy of the artist and David Castillo Gallery,
Miami

36. *My Song to Sing*, 2013
Ink, acrylic, paper, and fabric collage on
wood panel
84 x 84 x 2 in.
Private collection

37. *Like a Song*, 2010
Acrylic, fabric, and collage on panel
84 x 60 x 2 in.
Private collection

38. *Always and Everywhere*, 2013
Acrylic, ink, fabric, and collage on canvas
over panel
60 x 60 x 2 in.
Private collection

39. *The one that you love*, 2015
Clothing, linens, dog blankets, fabric, acrylic,
and collage on canvas over wood panel
64 x 49 x 3 in.
Collection of Sara M. and Michelle Vance Waddell

40. *Cathedral Street*, 2013
Clothing, pillow, wood, string, ribbon, and rope
19 x 26 x 17 in.
Courtesy of the Shlesinger-Walbohm Family
Collection, Toronto

41. *Daisies up your butterfly*, 2013
Clothing, fabric, and ribbon
12 x 12 in.
Collection of Sara M. and Michelle Vance Waddell

42. *Birdhouse of My Soul*, 2011
Acrylic, ink, fabric, and collage on canvas over
wood panel
84 x 120 x 4 in.
Private collection, Luxembourg

43. *My Belly Button Window*, 2016
Ink, acrylic, fabric, collage, ribbon, yarn,
and objects
66 x 78 x 6 in.
Courtesy of the artist and David Castillo Gallery,
Miami

44. *Where my heart grows*, 2016
Ink, acrylic, fabric, collage, and found objects
60 x 48 x 4 in.
Courtesy of the artist and David Castillo Gallery,
Miami

Photo Credits

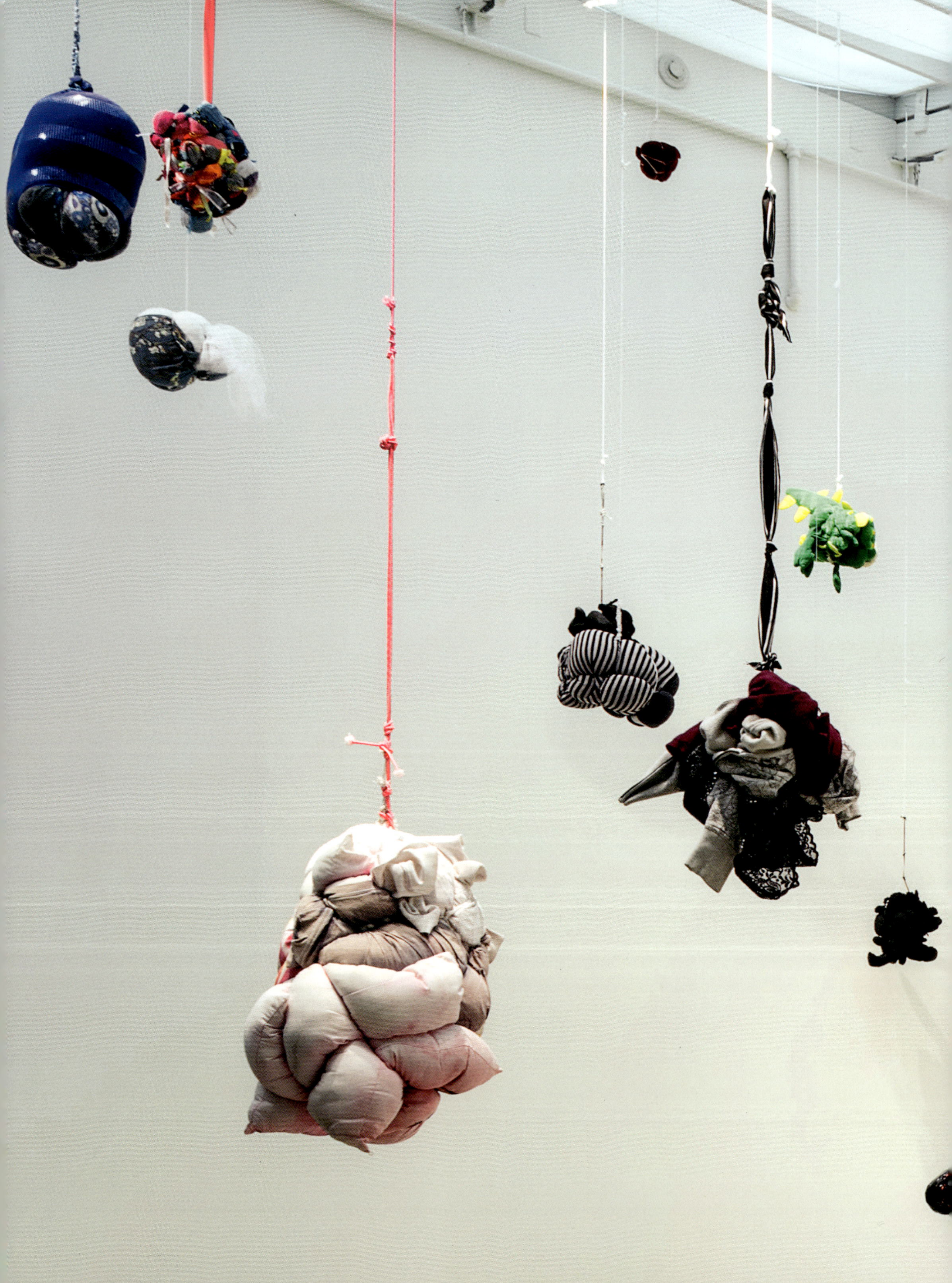